EMPATH
TO
SELF LOVE

A healing guide to compassion, sensitivity, and protection

Arlo J Lorenz

FeltIt InMyHeart Press

2

QUOTES:

"I LOVED this book! It is awesome and will be a game changer. Arlo gives positive practices to change and improve our lives as Empaths! I can't wait to suggest it to fellow Empaths, both empowered and struggling can benefit."

Larri Cook

"My favorite grounding read, I'm going to just carry it around with me."

Requested Anonymous

"This book gave me another angle to approach my life, and to sift out the negativity we all see."

Matt McKinnie

"I came away with a lot of positive vibes after reading it, coming out of the dark tunnel into the light to see the good in the world."

Patricia Lazik

"Arlo took on the most difficult of subjects and wrote a WINNER, this is the most valuable guide for a budding or blossoming Empath to become and stay good."

Requested Anonymous

FORWARD

I don't do readings, I'm not a life coach; in other words, in no way am I paid for this. I have no interest in Wicca, Religion, or casting spells. I've already written a book, so am under the impression I'll never make any money off this project and will be lucky to break even. In other words, I'm an unbiased third party without terms. My whole vested interest is that I am an Empath. Albeit selfish, my initial care was about maintaining my own energy levels well enough to live a beautiful life and create positivity with it. I'm an individual who, despite being dealt an arguably losing hand, pulled it all together and made a positive loving life. I've managed to figure this out, but not without a substantial painful process. My hope is to shorten that process for you.

I want you to find internal light that helps you lighten the load you carry, maintain balance, and create positivity with it. If there is one thing I know for sure about being Empathic, the tough parts cannot be discounted or marginalized. They must be addressed in order to truly live. With that said, I think it's also important to know that solutions are always dependent on the context of how the challenge is framed. You must go through the rough spots (walk through the fire) to find peace on the other side. Trying to run or go around results in a feeling of loss and emptiness. Then comes the addictive behavior, trying to fill the hole left behind. This strategy nearly cost me my life, leading me to believe that being an Empath has been the greatest honor, and greatest disaster, of my life.

I began writing this while still having questions about who and what I am. I realized that I knew much of what was out there, but I was still uncomfortable with how my mind interacted with others seemingly against my will. I learned a lot about who I am through my prior autobiographical book effort (*Saved with Honu*), and this led me to a level of understanding that allowed me to visualize this text. I am so very excited to tie all of this together for you. To illuminate for you a sense of control over something seen as uncontrollable is life affirming for the both of us.

With every major writing there are challenges. I put this book through an editing group. The feedback was consistent; "Share more of your story." "Put more of your personal context in there." I set out to write this away from my personal story because I'd already written an autobiography, and for the sake of length and making this a manageable read I chose to sprinkle a bit more in there, but leave it up to the reader to seek out my background if they would like. I'm not trying to sell you another book by any means, but this text seemingly takes on a bit more context with my autobiography in mind. One particular reader called this book a sequel, saying "You write from the heart, and that book lets people understand you, and your heart." It is my story and the ultimate why, so in that context, they do tie together.

Once you obtain additional knowledge of your situation and abilities, it's inevitable that you will rise to a greater state of enlightenment. This text is meant to allow you the knowledge and freedom to make this leap.

"Within the flood of life, one only has to increase their buoyancy to reach a higher state."

-Buddha.

Table of Content

INTRODUCTION

Let's be honest. In Western civilization, being an Empath is not a glamorous title. Generally, the Western Medical Society tries to medicate us all while insulting us with the title "crazy." What if I told you that this was all rubbish, you are not crazy, Western Medicine is the issue, and there is a centuries-old cultural and medical explanation for who you are as an Empath? Not only that, but that the explanation does not degrade you, but rather names you beautiful, wise, and one of the most important members to the balance and well-being of all living things, including the human race. I'll go on to tell you that the negativity that you may feel towards being Empathic is simply a lack of understanding, and through reading this text you will have the tools and courage to make changes. Through that process you'll understand why and how you are integral in the workings of society, and if you choose to, you may lead and balance the world in a way that you never thought possible. I know this is a bold claim, but I once laid helpless and suicidal on the dusty floor, unable to move, and if I can see the beauty in who I am, then you can see the beauty in who you are. I've written this book because I learned the hard way; I understand being an Empath, and I love you for who you are in this moment.

As a self-acknowledged Empath, you have a foot in the door of enlightenment. For you, this is a natural default. With everything in life there is an element of choice. Being an Empath is no different to an extent. Being empathic may be a core part of you, but turning it into being an Empath can be likened to an internal calling of maturation. In other words, embracing your Empathic nature, to become a true Empath may be the key to the best version of yourself. This may affect not only your own wellbeing, but the wellbeing of everyone you come in contact with. In a world that lacks an overall sense of courage, it is in itself a courageous act to love oneself. Being courageous in your path as an Empath is pivotal to your effectiveness, overall health, and wellbeing.

Let's get started

THE
CULTURE/THE
DARK

ABOUT THE AUTHOR

If I could go back and help myself - before the drinking, depression, suicidal thoughts, and loss of seven years of my life - I would. If I could somehow catch it so early that those challenges never surfaced, that's the gift that I want to give. I'm half a life old, but have only truly lived for the nine years leading to this text. Life is inevitably too short when you never truly live it. As Neale Donald Walsch said, "Life begins where your comfort zone ends." What if you never truly live? You may spend your whole life dying.

In writing this book, I always kept in mind my favorite quote. It comes from Lilla Watson, an Australian Aboriginal Elder: "If you have come to help me, you are wasting your time. If you have come because your liberation is bound up with mine, then let us work together." – I think this is beautiful, and it is simple in its explanation of the independent Empath and how an Empath fits into the collective of all. I'll repeat this quote at the end of this book, with the hope that you realize it's full context.

I've often found myself feeling that I'm without a culture of my own. I come from divorce, and this draws a sharp line down the center of my being. Both of my biological parents are Empathic, although neither is fully aware of what that means. With the absence of my Father, and until my Mother remarried my adoptive Dad, I was raised by a group predominated by women, made up of Grandparents and Aunts on both sides, and my Mother. This very Yin (Feminine) exposure increased my sensitivity. I then suffered an injury resulting in four major surgeries that again put me in touch with my emotional surroundings.

I was not raised as an Empath, or with any understanding of the things in this book. The contents of this book stem from the fact I am Empathic, and have a need to understand what and who I am. I attempted to run from those emotional surroundings, and it resulted in a seven-year depression that nearly cost me my life. I lost two-plus years of memory, and although I kept breathing through it all, I very much died. I successfully shut it off for years only to become suicidal. I was dead inside, and upon coming out of that depression came back to a half-life. When I was brave enough and grounded enough, I opened back up to find life again. "To live is the rarest thing in the world," said Oscar Wilde, but to understand this I unfortunately had to die.

I'm born of Western culture where the value of money is too high and celebration of the individual spirit too low. Because of this I've sought out the study of cultures that value and celebrate historical roots. I best identify with Native American culture because many Native American people are local to my birth location. I've had many friends from the Sioux tribe, and good exposure to celebration and tradition as allowed. The hardship of this culture is also similar to the Aboriginal Australian people. From a spiritual perspective I'm also attracted to the teachings of Buddha although I don't align myself to any religion. I love the concepts of Karma, Qi, Yin/Yang, and the study of Zen, and truly believe in the natural balance or Golden Mean to all things. I have no religious or political affiliation that can sway my independence, yet I feel connected to everything. I simply base my decisions on honesty, have surrounded myself with honest people as my best friends, and this works well for me.

Western society may be described as a melting pot, but does this come along with a loss of foundational knowledge? What I mean is that the cultures I study all have one thing in common, and that's a story. This story is passed down through generations, resulting in a personal peace and belonging as the individual knows their history. This further provides purpose and a sense of boundaries set by prior learning. Western culture is so infantile in comparison, and that often leaves individuals looking for a spiritual home, or even just basic knowledge of themselves. Much of the time we do not have a clear sense of purpose, nor the boundaries set by stories passed down by our elders. As Empaths, taking on this feeling of loss from others only compounds our own feelings, and we struggle to hold ourselves up against the combined weight of society's mental wellbeing.

I've taken this project on as there are a lot of seemingly disconnected pieces of information about being an Empath, but there is not a singular source I've found that addresses being an Empath with confidence. Much of the existing writing deals with the negative feelings of being an Empath, but the writings often leave out the profound potential that an individual of strong mind can accomplish. Those writings often lead to a personal perspective primarily based on feelings, but do not give foundation to the subject. Additionally, they are all about quick wins. There is little effort to find a long-term solution.

What I found while researching and quantifying my own experiences is that I had a lot of subject matter, but very little to hold it together. I likened it to a bunch of marbles rolling around on a tabletop. They rolled around, and although I could provide them direction at times, there was no way to hold them together and no bag to put them in. To find this bag for all of these marbles I went in search of older human experience writings. This search turned the entire text on a dime, and what I found was a long and rich historical presence of Empaths being known as healers, leaders, and "The Wise." In these writings, Empaths are known as the connective tissue of the greater human experience. I primarily found this in the context of Chinese Medicine, and although I'm not a doctor, I took an interest in the study of Chinese Medicine. This was first out of curiosity, but second to form the context of this book. The theory then grew into the text you have in your hands.

The goal of this book is to help you find yourself as an Empath. A knowledge of yourself that includes daily sanity and understanding of who you really are. Some days it's never enough, other days you have the strength to help others. Then there are the days were getting out of bed seems an impossible task. The rest of the days are a manic test of personal servitude mixed with a sense of compassion. Today is the day that you decide to favor the days where helping others is a possibility, for if this affliction has purpose, it's for you to have enough skill to bring yourself up and lead others in their like efforts.

WALKING THROUGH THE FIRE

Strength is a test of will, and will is a test of self-belief. You have the right to be strong, and it is an ongoing choice. Strength is predominantly a mental attribute, although there are physical aspects to it. The physical attributes that I speak of are not being able to bench three hundred pounds or run a six-minute mile. The ones that I speak of are a good immune system, healthy circulatory and respiratory systems, and regeneration of non-cancerous cells to name a few. It is a fact that we regenerate every cell in our body every two years, we should be doing everything in our power to ensure that those cells are healthy. I believe that the most powerful mental attribute is the ability to say "Yes" or "No" with honesty, and cognitive balance in a moment of weakness, to yourself and others.

Your mental strength and physical strength are tied in many ways. The mental foundations are honesty, positivity, and seeing troubles as opportunities rather than problems. The physical foundations are diet and exercise. It should be noted that in both mental and physical strength there is significant overlap, as exercise and diet also benefit the mental state, just as a peace and joy will benefit the physical state.

I commonly refer to the related opportunities for overall wellness as the "Fire in your life." The analogy incorporates the fear of being burnt, the pain that causes, and the instinctual need to go around, not through. As humans, we are programmed to avoid and survive to fight another day. If we take this path, we indeed survive, but we end up leading a half-life that is incomplete because those things we avoid hang over us as unresolved issues, introducing the potential for dependency and unintended pain. A personal mantra of mine: if you are willing to walk through the fires of your own life, you will inevitably become a leader to those who are not willing to walk through the fires in their own lives. You will be ahead and through the painful parts, stronger and more courageous, while they will still be avoiding the adversity, fearing the burn of facing a potential truth. The sad part is, those who have walked through the fire know that it looks worse than it is. They will testify that they really didn't get burnt in the process. Rather the opposite, they find relief through accomplishment. Trying to avoid the journey torments the soul far more than facing it head on.

Choice is your individual superpower; if your choices align with honesty, humility, integrity and responsibility, along with the practice of compassion and patience towards yourself first and others second, all challenges that you face in your daily life, with time will fade away. You will regain your balance, health, and most importantly self-reliance and respect. All things are curable, and compassion is the cure; helping others with like challenges is a way through the fire.

TRAITS OF AN EMPATH

My concern for the condition of the world is greater than the self-fulfilling interest of any single person. As an Empath, you are tuned into this by default. For instance, Empathic happiness is addictive and contagious. Studies have shown that being Empathic is real; if you have a friend who lives within twenty-five miles and you are happy, this person has a twenty-five percent greater likelihood to also be happy. Although this effect has been proven to diminish over space and time, it aligns with many people's Empathic experience.

There are many traits of being an Empath, but I believe that there is a single theory that overarches all of them. That is the concept of Hive Mind as it applies to being an Empath. The theory of Hive Mind is that an entire community of individuals share all experiences and knowledge of those experiences through one overreaching collective mind that connects each individual and their knowledge, to all other individuals and their knowledge. In short, Hive Mind is when each member of a species has constant awareness of the cumulative knowledge of the entire species. The very definition of being an Empath beckons to having Hive Mind capabilities. It's stated that empathy and compassion naturally attune your mind to another's, allowing mental activity exchange.

We connect with the world around us through our sensitivities. We react to them honestly, based on our minute by minute abilities. I've heard it through hundreds of sources that Empaths "just know." This indicates that we are picking up on an unseen vibration or frequency that allows us to know what someone else knows. I'm not saying that humans are capable of true Hive Mind, because we are not working as a collective toward the overall good of the community. I'm also not saying that being an Empath is limited to the confines of the human existence, as many of us have far greater connections with other animals outside of humans. With that said, could Hive Mind be an evolutionary potential to explore? What if as an Empath you've unlocked something, or, even more likely, retained something that allows you to access a different region, or even a greater percentage of your mind?

Over the years I've seen a lot of lists with varying traits of an Empath. Most of them are focused on the negatives. I've made every attempt to keep this entire text positive, including my list. I start this out with Genius, and I also think we should end it with Genius. Being Empathic is utilizing our hearts to understand, hear, and respond to our surrounding world. Genius is defined as using our whole intelligence. What we feel, and can impact is great, and we should be proud of that because it is Genius.

Traits of an Empath;

Genius – When an Empath is enlightened, and able to operate with courage, concentration, compassion, and integrity. There is a magical combination of knowingness and sense of peace that you bring to the world. This compassion, joy, and peace is impossible to be undone, has its own signature, and flows intact throughout time. A single Empath has the ability to uplift the entirety of society and to bring a powerful balance that people who are not in tune are incapable of. Within your genius, you may practice self-love, and through love, the art of healing others. Empaths are the gift the world so desperately needs.

Sense of Knowing – A very powerful intuition that is spooky and accurate about the personal wellness state of another living being or society. You feel like you know the person across the room. You sense their independent wellbeing, and, without intent, tie that to your own. You can sense vibrations in the world that are outside of the scientifically documented human senses. You have random bits of information graze your mind from unknown sources. You can tell when your friends are in pain, and somehow always call at just the right time. These are all indicators of being an Empath and the sense of knowing.

Caring – A need to care for and please others. Empaths have a tendency to take care of everyone around them, and sacrifice themselves in the process. You can feel the general wellbeing of others; this directly affects your mood and capabilities. On the other hand, you care for others and hope to make them feel well. This creates a situation where you attempt to bring others up through yourself. This can be in the form of compassion, but can also have personal costs and sacrifices. This creates circular patterns of behavior that can be both healthy and unhealthy. There is a personal benefit to Empaths for helping others, but there is a dividing line that must be drawn when that behavior begins to damage the self. Empaths attract people who are hurting (Empaths as a group label them narcissistic; this is a mistake). Those in pain are looking for relief and are drawn to the energy we produce, as we are working with our hearts.

1. Picking up the emotions of others. You feel sad or angry for no apparent reason. Your mood can change within the scope of a single breath without anything triggering it. If you're not able to track the feeling back to a logical internal state or feeling, you are picking this emotion up from someone else and may be channeling it as your own.

2. Taking on others' problems. You may be involved with someone facing a tough challenge and interject yourself, becoming so involved in formulating or finding a solution that you begin to own the issue as your own. Having a sense of control appears to be the solution, and this can temporarily yield personal truth, providing perspective concerning internal pain.

3. Taking on someone else's physical attributes or pain as your own. This is most famous as an attribute of a doting father-to-be taking on symptoms of their pregnant wife. This is as pure an Empathic response to love as you will find. You may feel the physical pain from others. We naturally connect with others by taking on physical attributes as an attempt to alleviate pain or circumstance.

Healer – Drawn to healing in all forms, metaphysical and spiritual. You naturally want to help others and protect yourself. Because of this you seek out solutions that will work for you. I've tried nearly everything, and this has led me to this writing. If you find yourself searching online for the spiritual and metaphysical properties of rose quartz then you personally know this one.

Food-Aware – In tune with the source of food and its path to your table, as well as its effects on your body. You sense the energy in foods, and as such Empaths have a tendency to lean toward being a vegetarian. Foods can calm, cool, and assist in feeling grounded and connecting back to the earth naturally.

Truth-Seeking – Uncovering the lie. You may sense the negativity of a lie and quickly turn on it to seek truth. Our hearts seek out truth. In our world of emotions, we are constantly in search of knowledge, and in the emotional world with little in the way of fact, we seek to ground and protect our hearts from harmful lies. Honesty is a cornerstone of being an Empath, for in honesty we find balance. The feeling of a lie creates negativity and chips away at our personal balance. You can feel the lie of another, and know when someone means to deceive you. You can also know an internal lie, and this ability can be used to know yourself and discern whether the thought or feeling you have is your own. Sometimes this is likened to that gut feeling or intuition taking on physical symptoms, such as digestive or lower back issues. These physical manifestations are often related to personal truth. If you are not living your own personal truth, your body may manifest pain to tell you to live honestly.

Dendrophile– Public places/cities are overwhelming. There is no distance where empathy and compassion expire. With that said, close proximity to large groups of people can be very overwhelming. This also relates to living circumstance; apartment or skyrise living can be detrimental. Depending on the strength of the ability, many Empaths pick up everything within 25 feet to 100 yards. Parties, Concerts, Malls, and Sporting events are some examples of venues that can feel like a bombardment of emotion.

Pacifism – You cannot tolerate violence or tragedy. In an age of school shootings, bombings, sport hunting, and terror attacks, Empaths have it hard. Sometimes it's just watching the news or a movie that digs at us. We are constantly looking for truth, peace, and balance, and are in natural servitude to it. Worldwide tragedies can cause us immeasurable personal pain, because we pull the personal reaction of society as a whole into our hearts and understanding. This can cause extreme loss of a personal nature. This can also manifest into physical pain taken on from others.

Dependence - Struggling with dependency and substance abuse is common among us. What may start as a lack of focus and getting lost in daydreams to shut off can quickly turn to drug seeking behavior to shut off. As an Empath, taking on the thoughts and feelings of others can weigh a person down, and shutting the mind off by passing out can sometimes feel like the only escape. I consider this the saddest factor, and it stems from an attempt to shut off the Empathic thoughts. Often this urge to escape turns to an addiction that hurts the self, a form of self-loathing that impacts many of us. Being clean and sober is fundamental to being able to embrace and cope with Empathic ability. This is a personal truth.

Spiritualist – Many Empaths live in a cluttered way, as organization feels heavy. They would rather embrace a free spirit way of moving through the world. This causes some disorganization of the things that hold less personal importance. The same thing can be said for rules that feel binding. Empaths are more oriented to the flow of the world, and emotions as a result. Rules feel like an unnecessary boundary to truth and honest intention.

Highly Creative, Artistic, Expressive – You find yourself creating for the benefit of others, or creating to calm yourself down. You find yourself keeping yourself busy in these ways to distract yourself and focus on positive things. Creative individuals are often Empathic; it allows us to connect with and portray the human experience, and this often comes out in an artistic form.

Good Listener, Bar Tender, Counselor – We should all admire those of us that can counsel others and spare themselves. Empaths have a natural ability to provide compassion, sympathize, empathize, and are often sought out as counselors, sometimes even by strangers.

Naturalist – Enjoys travel and wide-open spaces with little civilization; the city comes with a sense of depression and heaviness. You will always have connections with others that can span unlimited distances, but there is comfort in not being immersed in the feeling. Empaths enjoy the ability to feel direction and how they are traveling through the world based on magnetic poles. The best grounding that an Empath can seek out is simply getting away from the city, taking off your shoes, and standing in the grandeur of nature. This allows a connection to the greater self, feeds our need to decompress, and re-establishes roots to the mother earth.

Finally, I know it duplicates, but it's so worth saying again!

Genius – When an Empath is enlightened, and able to operate with courage, concentration, compassion, and integrity. There is a magical combination of knowingness and sense of peace that you bring to the world. This compassion, joy, and peace is impossible to be undone, has its own signature, and flows intact throughout time. A single Empath has the ability to uplift the entirety of society and to bring a powerful balance that people who are not in tune are incapable of. Within your genius you may practice self-love, and through love, the art of healing others. Empaths are the gift the world so desperately needs.

If you are reading this and are not naturally Empathic, you can still sense another through this process. Tune in to yourself, sense your breathing, body, and emotions; these acts prime your body to receive. Concentrate on the other person - their eyes, posture, and facial expressions. Relax and take in the physical cues, and you'll quickly become mindful of their bioelectric signal just under the surface.

As a natural Empath you are tapped into the collective of all experience. This is a lot to expect anyone to maintain, but once through the fire, your level of understanding of all life will provide such solace and peace that you'll not be able to see the world through the shades of yesterday.

CHINESE MEDICINE: FOUNDATIONS OF AN EMPATH

When I first tried to conceptualize this book, I had all of the symptoms of being an Empath, but no viable history. I needed to look further back into human experience learnings to find how an Empath can live a life of wellness. Empaths feel things that cannot be explained by textbook psychology or the norms of our society. With Western Medicine as a baseline, too many of us are being medicated with mood inhibitors simply because we can sense the wellbeing of a society, and that society does not conform to our needs. Defining an Empath through Western Medicine leads someone to be over-diagnosed. It's notable that the taking of a drug as prescribed by Western Medicine can very well become the disease itself. This is apparent in the opioid addiction statistics arising from the overuse of prescription pain medications. This also begs the question of the overall wellness of the society that we are able to sense.

Being an Empath tasks us with a large responsibility to honor ourselves, partly for our needs for personal wellness, but also as a vehicle for the betterment of society. I think it is also important to understand that Eastern Medicine does not see us as sick, it sees us for what we are: Empathic. Furthermore, there is a long-standing profile within Chinese Medicine that mentions our Empathic nature by name. This profile is the Heart profile (Heart network), and it is associated with warmth, compassion, healing, empathy, and love. There is an overarching sum of these traits adding up to wisdom.

Below are some of the reasons that Chinese Medicine fits our understanding of what an Empath is. Please take time to contemplate what is likely to be a stark contrast to Western Medicine and your personal experience as an Empath in the Western culture.

1. Chinese Medicine treats the person as a whole.

2. There is little place in Chinese Medicine for psychology. Concerns about mental wellness would be addressed as an imbalance in Yin and Yang.

3. Chinese Medicine sees all life as part of a greater union with nature. This relationship is reliant on the balance of Yin and Yang and its continual motion.

4. The vast majority of Chinese Medicine was founded upon practice on living patients. Death is revered as a next stage. The dead are not considered separated from the living, rather their energies are liberated from the binding of the body, and in relation have graduated to a more significant status as a ruler of the world.

5. The evolution of Chinese Medicine was maintained as knowledge obtained through trial and error and passed down over centuries, eventually combining into a medical practice.

6. The term Empath is used within the Heart profile, symbolizing balance within the heart. In Chinese Medicine, the heart is not only able to circulate Qi (Pronounced "Chee"), or your vital energy, but is also considered your internal wisdom, responsible for awareness, spirit, and life force. Your Heart is also considered your knowledge center, responsible for sharing your personal wisdom for the benefit of the world. The heart is known to have a memory center, and each beat of your heart generates a wave of energy felt around the world. This is why this text considers the Heart Profile a beautiful foundation for an Empath.

The minor role that psychology plays in Chinese Medicine is simply this: The overriding Empathic thoughts of Confucius concerning social order and well-being are central to the practice of philosophy/psychology in Chinese Medicine. It is considered that a productive, and well-adjusted person is a healthy person. This individual will be at harmony in their personal and productive lives. This philosophy confirms that strength is a product of freedom and harmony with nature. These thoughts affirm that all is related to Yin/Yang and the healthy movement of Qi as Life-force. This does not make room for Western psychology, which by principle dissects the individual to find the root of the issue. In Chinese Medicine it's the entire individual that is out of balance, and re-establishing that balance is the solution.

QI AS IT RELATES TO THE HEART

The phrase, 'my heart goes out to you' is literal in the case of Empaths. In Chinese Medicine, the heart is the knowledge source within the body, containing personal wisdom. It is also responsible for the distribution of your life force. This is embodied within the blood, and is called Qi. Your Qi is the energy, your internal wellness, the fire and spirit you transmit to others. Within the Heart profile of Chinese Medicine, when the spirit is strong, the individual is bright and balanced. They are loving and warm toward others. They have great ability to perceive the world through thought, communication, and memory.

When the spirit it weak, it's known to wander as if it has no comfortable place within the body, resulting in distraction, restlessness, and forgetfulness. When the spirit is absent, the individual is cold and cut off from society. This is a real challenge for people who are trying to cope with being an Empath rather than embracing who they really are. Often these people are stuck in toxic relationships, and struggle with sobriety because they don't exude the personal strength in the moment to create change. These individuals are hiding and just trying to make it through the day, but in place of positive constructive actions they are further injuring themselves and traveling farther away from their true nature, or personal sense of truth.

To live within yourself, you cannot be concerned with the impression of others or make attempts to impress others. Instead, make attempts to impress yourself, and those who are meant to will be naturally drawn to you. This way you remain secure, and the friends that are there are supposed to be there. I live a shortened version of this daily, and often recite, "The only person you need to impress today is you."

With that said, great imbalance is apparent when foundational Qi is stagnant (simply being alive) and healthy catalytic Qi (the forward nutritive motion and momentum created by a healthy life in balance) are at odds. We must move forward through balance, Yin/Yang, to produce the momentum to sustain our life force in a healthy and positive manner. Sickness is a representation of the body's inability to adapt, and one of the pitfalls of our society and Western Medicine is we are being forced to adapt at a compounding rate. Much of the time, the medicine provided is rooted in the very structure we are attempting to adapt to, which creates a cycle of inevitable illness. To be balanced within the Heart profile as an Empath is to be warm and embracing of the world and our personal knowledge. To be imbalanced is to be cold and shut off from our true nature as positive contributors to the betterment of the world.

The heart is also a communication device, as it's an extremely powerful generator of energy, creating our life force. This life force creates energy that progresses outwards from our bodies at the speed of light. We communicate through this method, because on a second by second basis your heartbeat communicates your Qi with every living entity on earth. To those people who we are closest with, our hearts have been shown to align in rhythm. It's also been shown that the Brain, Spine, and Heart come from the same embryological layer utilizing neural crest cells, and that as such they maintain their own form of memory. When someone you love in your heart feels something sad or exciting you are permeated with that feeling instantaneously through their heart. This is Qi and being an Empath. Not only is it natural, it's foundational.

Qi is the heat and continual movement of energy that makes up a body. This includes all mental and physical aspects of the body, and is described as one's life force. Qi is responsible for all dispersion of nourishment and the regulation of all of the systems within the body. Chinese Medicine looks for imbalances in Qi in an effort to diagnose and heal, and to maintain ideal operating functions. This is all in an effort to avoid the development of sickness. In the case where there is existing illness, the goal of Chinese Medicine is to halt and cure it, and to prevent further disharmony in Qi. When a body in discord is corrected and disharmony removed, the body will balance as if the condition never existed.

Qi is seen as the balance of water and earth. In that way we are all connected back to earth and through the earth each other. Our Qi can be viewed within the properties of water and its interactions with the earth. When clean and in movement, it delivers nutrients to the Earth. When contaminated or dirty, it's thick and does not move as freely. When still, it becomes stagnant and soiled with growth. When cold it becomes hard/frozen. When hot, it becomes volatile and boils. When touched by wind, it swells and bows. This is a simple representation of the statement, "all things require balance."

Another important way we are tied to our environment is through the sun as our energy source. In order for there to be balance and growth, we must have roots in the earth, nutrients from the water, and the heat and light of the sun. Just as plants fail when not receiving the necessary nutrients, our bodies can also fail based on nutrition and our reactions and perception of our surroundings. The greatest challenge of being an Empath is to maintain your wellbeing while remaining tapped into the greater collectiveness of the Earth as described above. You feel what you feel because we are all indeed a small part in the greater system of life. You have a gift that causes you to not draw the line between yourself and the greater collective so harshly. This is a natural harmony that you feel, and it's beautiful. The greater goal of this book is to connect to that harmony, and make us all stronger in the process.

This all comes together as our emotions shape our bodies upon the generation of thoughts and feeling about ourselves and surroundings. If they are contrary to our overall wellbeing, our bodies will show this cost over time. This can be difficult for the young to understand. The young take their bodies for granted, but truth be told, the decisions made for today have long lasting consequences in the form of mental health, pending addictions, and overall disharmony. One poor decision leading to devastating circumstance can forever change the perception of the world, leading to the body's decline. This is why choice becomes important, as our futures are solely dependent on the choices made in the present.

YIN/YANG

The space between Yin and Yang is where Qi thrives. Yin, Yang, and Qi are always one entity in continual movement, and are commonly represented as the Taijitu (spiral energy, and the image that we are so familiar with). Qi has also been discussed by the Greeks as Phi, the Golden Mean, or Rule of thirds. To discuss the Golden Mean we will look to Yin and Yang, for the space between them is where balanced choice and understanding reside. Within my research I've found that in many circumstances two cultures with little exposure to each other will speak about the same concept. This is true of the Golden Mean and Taijitu. Anytime two cultures speak of the same concept I see this as a known Universal Truth. The best of life is found in the balance between Yin and Yang, and these teachings apply to every segment of life.

Youth is to Yang as Elderly is to Yin.

Heat is to Yang as Cold is to Yin.

Light is to Yang as Dark is to Yin.

Judgement is to Yang as Forgiveness is to Yin.

Erratic is to Yang as Calm is to Yin.

Male is to Yang as Female is to Yin.

Yin and Yang form a cyclical relationship that is individually dependent on perception. It is the cycling and balance of any life. Yin and Yang are made up entirely by their relation to each other and cannot be separated. The little space between Yin and Yang is where Qi survives and is in tune, where all things are in balance. As an example, there is no dark without light. There is no death without birth. There is no heat without cold. There is also a distinction to make in that day does not cause night, birth does not cause death, and heat does not cause cold.

You are also balancing other entities. Sometimes you know of them, other times strangers are reliant on you. This is also not a one to one relationship, as a small amount of light defeats a great volume of dark. Similarly, the positivity and compassion in one Empath balances many more individuals in The Dark (discussed in detail later in this text) on a compounding scale. Most of us Empaths are subject to the shortfalls of Yin, as we stay in the shadows and have become cold and quiet through the process. I'm no exception. The Dark feeds on our insecurities and we feel inadequate to make necessary changes. It is possible to gain more Yang through increased energy and expansion in the way of courage to try and experience new things.

I'm going to take a moment and mix cultures with an old Native American Indian story that beautifully represents Yin and Yang. A Native American elder woman was once asked in her old age how she became so wise. Her response was simply that she had two Wolves in her heart, the Wolf of Love and the Wolf of Hate, and that she became so wise by feeding the Wolf of Love more than she fed the Wolf of Hate. The Wolf of Love is Yin and the Wolf of Hate is Yang. What amazes me is that this same wisdom spans different cultures (Chinese, Greek, and Native American to name a few) on different continents that at the time would have had little exposure to each other. This is the sign of a Universal Truth.

Our ability to feed the Wolf of Love is core to our ability to remain strong, and if we are not approaching this with a sense of purpose, we will fall victim to our Wolf of Hate. Our Wolf of Hate may resemble negative self-speak, or putting someone else down in their time of need to make ourselves feel better. For those that do not feel the anguish of the world, feeding the Wolf of Hate often escalates into physical violence based on attributes of The Dark.

Feeding the Wolf of Love is to our nature, it feels good, we want to balance ourselves and others, but we often find our intention focused on others before ourselves, making our intentions weak and half-hearted. It's important to remember that our Wolf of Love is first internal, and must be approached with compassion and kindness as you would expect to approach any wolf if not wanting to be devoured by it. Once pacified internally, the Wolf of Love can be courageous on behalf of others and is stronger than The Wolf of Hate. The intention should be to reduce the quarrels of your internal Wolves. With daily feeding of your internal Wolf of Love, it should be obvious that the Wolf of Hate stands no chance. With great strength, your single Wolf of Love can stand up to packs of external Wolves of Hate (yours and scores of others) and win with ease.

There must be a realistic view of the Wolf of Hate. Regardless of how strong our Wolf of Love may become, there is no killing the Wolf of Hate. This is why forgiveness is the way, and judgement is foolish. This may also be attributed to Yin (forgiveness) and Yang (judgement). If we were to kill our Wolf of Hate, or even make the attempt, this would create the very thing you are trying to destroy through an overpowering act of Yang. The Wolf of Hate is void of empathy, but we must have empathy for it, because it is a part of us. Self-compassion and kindness soothe all, including our own Wolf of Hate.

Say, for instance, we were to attempt to kill our Wolf of Hate. We would then take a malicious and violent act toward the Wolf of Hate (judgement), only sacrificing our Wolf of Love (forgiveness) in the process. You would become weaker, fall out of balance, reside in The Dark. Once you discontinue the practice of love, you harm yourself. If you sever your connection to love, then you lose the ability to receive it, and fear takes over your life. Without a change to your current state of thought towards internal balance and compassion towards the Wolf of Hate, you may never find peace again, embracing a life of torment and violence (judgement) without sight of hope (forgiveness). The key is balance and awareness of our natural tendencies, and the daily choice to feed the Wolf of Love.

Being an Empath – is it a blessing or a curse? All states of being can be classified into Yin and Yang; Being an Empath is both Yin and Yang, so in likeness to Yin it's a blessing, in likeness to Yang it's a curse. But remember, Yin and Yang is based in a perception of that relationship between forces at odds with each other, and we are looking for the place where Qi thrives, otherwise known as the Golden Mean. This, like all other relationships between odds will ingest what you feed it, so looking upon it with a perspective of Yin, or positivity, will cast light upon it. It's incredibly personal because health is defined as the balance of Yin and Yang. Denying yourself compassion or running from being an Empath brings your Yin and Yang into imbalance. This denial only damages your Qi, and will have long term effects on your health and wellbeing.

Health is the balance of Yin and Yang, and sickness a result of the imbalance through deficiency or excess. In Western terms, an imbalance causes a weakened immune system, and the body is susceptible to attack and sickness. If the imbalance is not corrected the illness will root and progress, running its own cycle of Yin and Yang. It is up to the individual to maintain this balance (physical and mental) against formidable causes of illness, such as stress. In everyday life, the balance can be sought by providing for the self (Yin) in the world of our surroundings (Yang). This is why the Heart profile ties so closely to people who are Empathic, and also provides a long-established medical reason for who we are. So many of us feel crazy, but we are not crazy. We are enlightened, but not balanced in a way to reach our full potential. In order to live, we must see it as the Chinese culture has, and not in the way of Western Medicine which dissects our very essence into a chemical compound in a small bottle that we are instructed to take. This pill then only further damages the very life force, Qi, that we are trying to protect.

All too often we are trying to protect this life force as a mode of survival and not from a place of love. If we are in survival mode the decisions that we make in those moments, are the ones that set the foundations for the rest of our lives. If we are to run from ourselves, we will weaken our individual spirit and allow our life-force to wander. In order to truly live with our spirit bright and intact, we must come to terms with who we are as Empaths. It is our call to share the wisdom of the world through our luminous heart line. In doing this we will be seen as warm, enlightened, and steady, maintaining balance in ourselves and teaching others to find their spirit as well. We do this through benevolence, spreading joy, encouraging peace, and working through communication as our medium. The network already exists, and you are already online.

In addition to Qi, there are two energies spoken of within Chinese Medicine. We will not spend much time on them, but they, too, balance each other. Jing is the active body, and its ability to surmount and achieve without injury. Shen is the internal spirit, strength, and personality.

GETTING THE HEAD AND THE HEART TO WORK TOGETHER. THE YIN/YANG OF BEING AN EMPATH.

As Empaths, we often lead with our hearts. This is our greatest strength, but may also be our greatest weakness when not balanced with what I call the heart/head balance. If we lead with our hearts too much, we may only think about our own well-being when faced with personal pain. This can set in upon the realization that we've gotten ourselves into a situation that we feel we can no longer control. This is especially difficult when we are trying to help the less fortunate but are unable to accumulate the personal resources to do so. We then may feel inadequate where we should instead be focusing on the positivity of the effort. We may also find ourselves in bad relationships because we had the best of intentions to help someone who is imbalanced. We think that we can "fix them." This is a very sticky situation, because only the individual can take responsibility for themselves. You cannot make choices for them. As leading with the heart is our natural inclination, we must then focus on leading with the head at times.

Leading with the head for us is taking a pause to think about our situation prior to rushing in. It's a moment to trust our intuition, slow down the process, listen to our emotions, and balance our individual well-being prior to rushing in. This can all happen within a second, but that second can provide great clarity concerning personal care within any situation.

There is such a thing as an Empath leading with the head too much. In our case, this is when we have pulled away from society in distrust, when we have analyzed everything as a threat and begin to lock ourselves away in an effort to protect ourselves. If you are drinking or using drugs in an effort to escape it all, count yourselves amongst them, and please realize that you are currently in The Dark. This is not a permanent state of consciousness, but rather a stepping stone to opportunity. This is a fear response, and at this point we need to embrace choice with our hearts. We need to turn to ourselves with compassion and love to get strong enough to be our true selves.

The point is, we must be careful in our choices so that we may remain balanced and do our potential good as only a beautiful balanced Empath can. The positive or negative situations are a springboard for personal growth and development. Leave the self-limiting thoughts in the past and move forward into positivity and healthy relationships with yourself and others.

THE DARK

Life with purpose (doing good for others) can never lose meaning; lives that seem without purpose are lived in the shadow of depression, dependency, and suicidal tendencies. All lives can be more fruitful. There is no medication that can fix depression or suicidal thoughts, as they are derived either through the internal or external destructions of a life. It remains a personal level of choice and attitude towards our past that either allows us to move forward or holds us in the past. A life without meaning (one stuck in the mode of survival) is a life without the ability to create a dream. This is what I define as The Dark, and The Dark haunts our ability to dream, and therefore haunts our ability to create our path. The Dark is created by your own mind focusing on the negative (a problem), the past (a slight or trauma), or an imagined terrible outcome (stress, and worry resulting in anxiety). Sadly, when we are in The Dark, we expend incredible amounts of energy on judgement, resentment, personal numbing, and suffering.

The lowest form of human spiritual evolution is Shame; the highest, Enlightenment. There are far more individuals suffering in shame than those who are enlightened, but as each level radiates at its own frequency the few enlightened can counterbalance the masses suffering in shame.

"If you want love, be loving. If you want peace, be peaceful. If you wish to see joy, be joyful."

Mahatma Gandhi

The Dark vs Enlightenment is equivalent to the stories of old where good prevails over evil and light over darkness. With that said, good/evil, light/darkness will naturally balance as discussed in Yin/Yang. This leaves many in The Dark, and few strong individuals in The Light, as light has far greater power. Think of this in terms of fireworks - the darkness is necessary.

Fireworks' piercing light against the backdrop of the dark can be seen from a great distance, and from any direction. You may be one of the millions in the dark, just looking for a bit of light. My hope for everyone is that they can find a way to be The Light. It's inside all of us, as proven by the fact that the human body emits light as a byproduct of Qi. Making this light known to yourself and others is a step in becoming your best self.

I would like to speak about the laws of Karma, because it has direct correlation. The frequencies that you are most likely to receive as an Empath are those that you put out. Karma is: you reap what you sow, you attract what you radiate, you get what you give, and your strength is based on your choices. Good begets good, and evil begets evil. Positivity attracts positivity and wisdom. Negativity attracts ignorance (most commonly as entertainment). You will be more apt to receive the vibrational frequencies that you produce. The point is if you want to take on less of the hurtful pieces of being an Empath, working through the path to love and enlightenment is the only permanent solution. You can always expect your input from society to be approximately what your output is to others. This is Karma and Yin/Yang all wrapped into one.

Let's understand The Dark, so that we may begin to make strides to The Light. Empaths have the ability to accept energies in various forms: emotional, physical, spiritual, nutritional, etc... The key is to learn to manage these energies, gain education about ourselves and know that healing is derived from self-wellness. No one can truly heal another person, but we can influence mood, and temporarily take some of the negativity from another individual's aura or personal state. This is in the form of transference, so what you take you must also rid yourself of. This can lead to others feeding off of your positive energy in exchange for their negative and vice versa. It's important to understand this dynamic in your relationships. If they are one–sided, negative for your positive, you may feel drained by the relationship and seek out cord cutting as a method of separation. If the other individual is receptive, you may be able to give them tools and show them the way to balancing and producing the results of self-care.

The easiest way to see Karma in Western culture, and yes, it's alive and we pay large sums of money to experience it, is through nearly every superhero movie script ever written. The hero of light is set against insurmountable odds, somehow finds a way to battle their internal doubt, and finds a way to prevail, thus restoring hope and peace to the world. That's fantastic, and extremely predictable in the current age of cinema, but we always show up. The truth of the matter is that far too often we show up for the drama created by the villain rather than the heroism of the hero. This is Yin/Yang, and the villain is always the subject of their own Karma, sealing their defeat in their own darkness. The hero enjoys good fortune, celebration for their positivity, and a sort of invincibility that comes along with The Light. The villain is left to the dark, always plotting, but ultimately too weak to fully execute and win. Our entire culture shows up for and feeds on the drama of the villain, and unfortunately, it's about the dollar (our vote) in the form of ratings.

The news is awful and generally slanted towards The Dark. Take a moment and count news stories in any given hour. I'll bet that once done you'll find a one to four ratio of positive to negative, and this is in our information cycles. We are paying for it all of the time; you are voting with your dollars so it's chosen exposure. You may be saying, "Yes, but we know the hero prevails." This is true in the fact that we have written the script this way, but how often do plans match reality, and what is the cost? Then there's the obvious questions: if we supported The Light, and did not celebrate The Dark in the form of entertainment, would we be in this predicament? We've seen this before, it's history repeating, but most readily recalled is the Roman Empire which celebrated blood sport and became famous for "Are you not entertained?" Are we any different in our depictions in the name of profits?

I'll continually speak of walking through the fire of life throughout this text. This is an analogy for facing the obstacles as challenges rather than trying to avoid them. To face them head on is to walk through the fire, and we gain strength in the process. To avoid them is to sink deeper into your troubles and become weaker. Walking through the fire is how you climb the ladder from The Dark to Enlightenment. To walk through the fire of life will inevitably make you a leader to those who try to avoid their challenge in life. Being Empathic is one of those challenges. You can walk through this fire and come out the other side.

What is your why? Why do you fear being an Empath? Why do you use drugs, alcohol, or unhealthy relationships? Once you know your why, you know your weakness. Once you know your weakness, you can change your perspective on that weakness and turn it into a strength through self-work, hope, and compassion. This will be your fuel to escape The Dark. It can happen in an instant or take years, but if you are positive and seek personal and relational support systems, you can make it to a beautiful and strong life full of healthy relationships and personal abundance.

David R Hawkins originally published the Map of Consciousness, and the following are my take on those attributes in the order originally published. Out of these attributes, Shame has the lowest resonance and Pride has the highest. Even though they are progressive, each building upon the prior, these attributes make up The Dark. I would also like to admit that I've experienced all of these levels personally. I know the requirements of the progression; it's being kind, first to yourself, then to others. That's the grand secret. Of course, it's not that easy, and the remainder of this book will focus on defining the challenge and presenting tools, perspectives, and tricks to navigate the solution.

Shame - Mentalities that are based in Shame are generally in a state that does not actively take precautions to provide sustenance or prolong their own life. This may result in the purposeful taking of their own life and/or the lives of others. I want to make it very clear that suicide is not an option for you. I'm a survivor of these thoughts, and you will be too.

Guilt - Guilt is a negative attitude that holds the person in an unforgiven state. This is a perpetual prison and the individual is the only person that can find the key. Often times they hold the key in their own hand and refuse to unlock the door for the feeling that they deserve to be there. This is a place devoid of self-compassion, but, as you will learn, forgiveness and compassion are necessary to move forward. It's also a state of inaction, for if we are wronged, we will no longer lodge a complaint. Many people in this place take out their frustrations on others in violent outbursts and public criticism. They are externalizing their own feelings about themselves, but have little ability to make that connection. If you are doing this, stop and think about your why. Take all the time you need, but forgive yourself as soon as possible.

Apathy - Apathy is a general inability to take action for lack of hope that anything will improve. Often it takes an intervention to break out of the cycle of sorrow, as there will be little or no activity in the individual's life. There may be a fixation, and a singular thought process that always leads back to its origin and begins again, causing the individual to become cold or stuck in life.

Grief - Even the strongest of individuals may find themselves struck with grief. Whether caused by major trauma or a loss of love in an individual's life, there is a possibility of being stuck in grief. There is a lack of trust and a focus on a feeling of emptiness in place of a willingness to try and move forward. People often arrange their life in a way to avoid risk, vulnerability, and passion.

Fear – A feeling and viewpoint of the world that everyone and everything is out to get them. This person actively avoids risk. Shut-in people who have limited social contact and are stuck in their own homes is an extreme example of these individuals. These individuals appear stuck in place and unable to move due to the perception that there are dangers around every corner. I know many Empaths that get stuck here. To counteract empathic tendencies, they try to shut it all out and lose their self/self confidence in the process. They lose their entire lives to a fear of living. It's important to know that you are not the external thoughts that live inside you, and with the ideas in this text you can build away from and separate those thoughts from who you really are.

Desire – A focus on the accumulation of material items that have a lot to do with greed. These people have a lot of stuff and claim that their stuff makes them happy. These individuals are in it for the rush, and thus are subject to addiction. Additionally, they will put themselves in danger to please others. This may include irresponsible sex and drug use. They are often the life of the party, but when that party is over, they sink into a feeling of emptiness.

Anger – A frustration based in want for a level of treatment or a material item that seems out of reach. This individual may do anything to obtain this item or the level of respect desired, and may resort to violence through force in order to obtain a desired result, even if it's short term. These people may be wearing a mask in their daily life, but if pushed, react with an unstable, impulsive, emotional state, and physical or vocal outburst.

Pride - Economic and material desires lead, at best, to pride. Pride is a source of rightness, and ultimately society pays the cost of pride. Pride often empowers the military of a group or entity, as these individuals are willing to take orders and sacrifice the wellbeing of themselves and others. Due to this, pride is responsible for the holocaust, wars, and terrorism. Individuals embodying pride often appear tight and well-mannered, but will be passionate about their ability to be right, and will not concede their position.

PITFALLS OF THE DARK

Fearful fact - Fear is inherited. Once we have fear, we also place it on others. This is inherited fear. Take, for instance, a young child aware of a storm outside. As a parent you say, "Don't be afraid of the storm." Although you intend this to be supportive, you just implanted the idea into the child that fear of the storm is a real and viable option. You see this in family dynamics all the time. It's common in media, sports, eating habits, relationships, spoken language, and most noticeably overall confidence. We reproduce in our families our own fear, whether we realize it or not. Fear is in our verbal DNA and permeates every facet of society. This is one reason why the media has such power; it reinforces what we've been taught to expect with most of our worldly interactions.

Anger - Imagine for a moment operating in anger all of the time. Friends would dissipate, you'd make all of your apparent problems worse by alienating your support system, and your health would slowly fail due to a buildup of adrenaline and acidity in your body.

Pride - Rightness is a foundation of falsehood. The need to be right has created everything from war, holocaust, and genocide, to famine under the guise of a government unwilling to help its own people due to corruption and greed. I'm unable to think of a single situation where the need to be right has left a long-standing, positive impact on the human existence, and that's not to discount all of the destruction that it's caused to the world and all its species. In short, Rightness is the enemy to internal and external balance and peace. It's usually based on greed, ego, want, and the obsessive collection of material items. Rightness only postures us for falsehood and inevitable loss.

A negative world view, in the long term, will cause addiction and pain through illness. If residing in a negative world view, our bodies will show this over time. Sadly, by the time illness is detectable within the realm of Western Medicine, the illness has built a foundation and is building upon itself to the point of necessary intervention. Worry, falsehood, and negativity destroy the foundations of our body by making our immune systems weak and our bodies frail. There is no expected recovery from a negative world view and its devastating effects on the body and mind other than a significant change in outlook leading to a significant change in personality.

This change requires walking through the fire of fear and addiction to find the courage to start again. This rebirth will be in the name of courage, honesty, and integrity, and will lead to health and wellbeing that you may not have experienced since childhood. This same courage is an insurance policy against future circumstance that may shake the foundation of your new-found positivity. By remembering that love concerns all, and that our attitude toward the situation is key, we can weather the storm of life when our belief systems are shaken, and make our personal recoveries incredibly short. If we are to take the pain and lessons in life, and with courage and a sense of humility overcome them, then they have not been wasted, but rather became the vehicle for which we walked through the fire to become leaders in our own right.

Furthermore, our true capabilities are all linked to our health. If you don't feel well, if you are wallowing in self-doubt, your ability to understand, forgive, and provide compassion to yourself and others will be hampered. Improving your physical health will improve your mental state and vice-versa. How you choose to experience life effects your body's composition, and we will expand on this greatly through the scientific section of this text. For now, know that your attitude and choice to live with anabolic endorphins connects to your organ systems through the body's meridians calming the organ systems. Laughter instills a sense of peace, which allows freedom and acceptance to circumstance.

NARCISSISTS

By definition, narcissism is gratification yielding from vanity, ego, and admiration of one's idealized self-image and attributes. The online article base labels all individuals who impact Empaths in a negative way Narcissists. Because of this, through the next two chapters I've written with the term as a point of focus. Foundationally, I do not like that as Empaths we have labeled a group of individuals Narcissists, because labels require judgement. I'm forced to write utilizing the label as reference because it's so prevalent in our circles. The term Narcissist, or even Energy Vampire, is a continual topic. I don't like labels for the simple reason that it creates an Us vs Them complex, and, with it, conflict.

With this said, when you hear the term "Narcissist," I challenge you to engage in a recoding exercise and pause to think; "People who cause me pain." Take the time to consider if this phrase fits the situation, or people who you associate with "Narcissist" more accurately. Within the phrase "People who cause me pain," there is less room for judgement, and more room for forgiveness resulting in greater potential for personal freedom. This recoding also allows for separation from the Us vs Them mentality and group labeling.

Narcissism in Western culture is an expectation given to us by society and the media. Considered a social problem, narcissism is based off an imagined perfect look or perfect life that becomes an expectation rather than a personal goal. We see this in the way that people filter their social media posts to make their lives seem blissful. The flaw is that people we commonly see as narcissistic don't work towards this goal, but rather wish for it. When it does not turn out as imagined, they refuse to take personal responsibility and blame others.

Common characteristics include being without the ability to feel personal shame and being quick to judge others, as well as imagined perfection of themselves and the lives that they lead. They need to inflate their own ego at the expense of another individual. This may stem from envy, jealousy, or guilt, and often leads to an attempt to exploit others for personal gain and an inability to recognize boundaries, often linked to a sense of entitlement. If lofty expectations that they place on others are not met, they place blame, as there are no boundaries between the perceived self-need and the external expectation.

Empaths are magnetic for these individuals because their internal image is not the image that they are portraying to the world. The narcissistic image requires buildup and maintenance, and who better than an Empath, who is sensitive, caring, and willing to put themself second, to build yourself up upon. The weak will love you for it, and you'll probably get some of your needs met too, until you stand up for yourself and place your needs ahead of theirs. If they view you as subservient to their needs, they will often lash out abruptly and begin to manipulate with blame and spite.

At some level, we are all narcissistic; societal expectations require it, and our overall society is becoming more narcissistic (you can thank social media for that one). Empaths who are trying to assist others before themselves will run into a challenge, because, in our society, there are many who will take advantage of others to feel better about themselves. When results are not tied to effort, we run the risk of creating individuals who maintain low self-esteem for lack of personal accomplishment. Similarly, Narcissists are a catch twenty-two of sorts, unwilling to do the work because they consider themselves perfect, and personally destructive for lack of accomplishment at the same time. This is one of the great flaws with this generational trend. What have we done about it? We've predominantly made fun of it, placing shame. Shame is a very low energy field, and the fact this is our go-to response is a sign of the well-being of our current society. This is why, as Empaths, we need to be stronger, not only for our own sake, but for the betterment of the world.

Being able to feel these individuals and their negative alignments, up to and including suicidal thoughts, is our greatest conflict. As much as you yearn to help them, you are no good to them in a weakened state. You must be able to practice self-love before you can come to the aid of others and truly assist them in understanding how to pull themselves up (if willing to do the work). You will then be stronger for the process of walking through your personal fire, and will be able to mentor them through the process, therefore giving back in an act of love. Think of it this way, you can't give something away that you don't have. Love conquers all, and love heals. You must first have it for yourself to be able to assist others in instilling it in themselves. I'm not saying that two people can't rely on each other and pull each other up simultaneously, but I am saying if one person slips, the weight of their fall may be enough to drag both individuals back down.

It's no wonder that Narcissism is commonly addressed within the online knowledge base about being an Empath, and in particular how to cope with it. It's the lowest hanging fruit there is to write about and can be recreated endlessly from different angles. If you take personal account of the people in your life, including a good hard look at yourself, it's easy to realize that we are all narcissistic. Much of this is aligning with social standards that have been forced upon us, but something as simple as a job interview requires us to become momentarily narcissistic. Then, if we receive the job, we must continue that line, and that's simply to make a living and provide for our loved ones.

TODAY'S SOCIETY

Within the scope of this chapter, I've written my thoughts on society and the flaws therein. The first of the following societal flaws is truly difficult to work around because it's a foundation of society. The overall argument is that many of the expectations of society damage the solitude and retention of the individual spirit. These are things that we should be aware of in natural servitude to our own spirit and how we align our expectations to society. We should also know that we cannot change the society itself on a day to day basis, but we can manage our expectations and reactions. In this way we can protect our spirit and sense of personal power on an ongoing basis.

Societal flaw one:

We dwarf the emotions of our youth and enforce societal norms at young ages. This starts with language, which is the first instance in which we dwarf Empathic communication. We then continue this line of thinking through child rearing, and as parents we enforce a silent set of rules in public that tells our children that expressing themselves is negative. This also places fear into our children, and an impossible standard/expectation to fit in. We inevitably internalize this, and begin to bottle our emotions. These emotions cause us nearly all of our pain, resulting in unresolved conflict that our imaginations apply to all situations, and we begin to shelter against unreal threats in place of trusting others. This continues through school years, and cliques and gangs determine the personality of a group rather than honoring the personal spirit of the individual. We lose our ability to stand alone and resolve conflict without a group. Even then, conflict resolution often becomes rooted in violence. We lose ourselves, and once the group dissipates due to the inevitable changes in life, we feel lost and have to "find ourselves" again. We go through the pain of rediscovery in an attempt to honor our independent spirits rather than retaining it all along. There are, of course, exceptional good friends that know and honor us, but all too often we allow the perceived strength of the group to overshadow our spirit and needs, and we choose the group over ourselves, losing ourselves in the process. This can be especially dangerous when the core family group is not close-knit and we define family as the friend group.

The result is that when someone goes through something painful, they end up thinking "No one could possibly know how I feel." The truth is, we all go through things that are very difficult, and most people that you meet on the street can relate in some way. We've been taught to bottle this and not talk about it. I'm no exception. Even though I've written my early story as an autobiography, I don't speak about my struggles in public unless invited to do so. Mainly because there's nothing more awkward than sitting down to lunch with your coworkers and leading conversation with, "Hey, did you know I was once suicidal and lost two years of memory within a seven-year depression?" The good thing is, I write what I need to hear, and by doing so I've healed myself and countless others. People who have read my story will commonly come up to me and say "I had no idea!" I smile and nod, comfortable in the knowledge they no longer feel as alone, and then I invite questions. Those questions rarely surface, because we've been taught to not talk about our emotions. By doing this, we instill fear into our youth, fear of their own emotions, and especially the ability to hold a conversation about the substance of their emotions. This then becomes a foundational baseline for the other societal flaws discussed below.

Societal flaw two:

We idealize image, we glamorize destructive lifestyles, we feed off drama and violence in the media and entertainment. We don't celebrate differences as we should, and we do celebrate similarities. In short, we celebrate negativity. The true high standard is a lack of drama through honesty, education, and a personal peace that causes one to only step outside themselves for a benefit to the collective. It's not worth going through the process of fitting into society only to lose the gift of enlightenment. This was once my fate, but I've realized that, for many, being enlightened is like the professor that looks at everyone in a class and says, "You all start with an A, it's up to you to keep it." You have to do the work, and as discussed above, this is outside of the realm of current possibilities for many. You must earn your rewards.

Societal flaw three:

Western culture conditions people through the media to become Narcissists and addicts. Commercials portray an ideal image that is not obtainable, but rather airbrushed. Addicts are pushed all kinds of products, including but not limited to food (sugar), and are given unlimited opportunities to buy something that will make them feel better. Then we have the news. For every positive covered there are four negatives.

My favorite are the drug commercials. Everyone looks so happy, and they are living a great life, but you're mesmerized by the image, not the message. Close your eyes and really listen to all of the side effects. It's amazing the contrast. We are being lulled into this feeling that life should be easy, because there's a happy ending to every story that we've ever been told. The trouble is, we are writing our own story. We feel like it should turn out like those on the TV, but without it being grounded in our reality, and without any of the actual work that it takes to get there. Narcissists and Empaths take in the same message, but fundamentally want a different solution. Both need to do the self-work to get the results that they want, and each is responsible for their results. This is the price of true freedom.

Societal flaw four:

Diffusion of responsibility shows up in two forms in our society. The first form is an unwillingness or lack of ability to help. Imagine this: an individual is being mugged in the courtyard of a busy apartment complex. They are screaming and yelling for help, and many people have opened their windows and walked out onto their patios to witness the crime. Each of these people also notices the others looking on. Each of these people thinks, "I should call 911 to report this and get this individual help." Each of these people fail to make the call because they assume that someone else will do it, so they don't have to. No help arrives, and the victim is hurt far worse due to the inaction.

The other way this shows up falls in line with the narcissistic culture that we are a part of as an inability to take responsibility for one's actions. There is a fairytale that we tell ourselves that it cannot be our fault because we have all the answers and are ultimately perfect. We then reinforce this endlessly because we want to be right. The truth is, we create 100% of our own problems, either by action or perception.

Societal flaw five:

Our society will almost always choose the path of least resistance, even if it's not the most beneficial path for our long term health and wellness. We regularly trade both our mental and physical health for ease of life on a societal level. We do this for two reasons: first it's easier, second it's more comfortable (in the short term). I make this point due to a personal health and wellness realization. I've suffered from a disability for nearly my entire life. For the longest time, I relied on the treatment of Western Medicine to the dismay of my mind and body. This was first out of convenience, then out of ignorance. When I was younger it was also easier to go to the doctor, get a prescription, and pop a pill than spend the same amount of money and hours at the gym and focused on a healthy diet. I was sick all the time, weak, dependent on the medicine, and imbalanced both physically and mentally. Pursuant to taking the path of least resistance as a society, we've made the decision to trade our health for comfort and convenience. This is readily seen in our massive consumption of fast food alone. We'd rather spend more money to get a daily vitamin than eat in a way where our dietary requirements are met. It's easier to take a pain pill, so we do that, putting ourselves at risk for addiction in place of gaining strength and releasing our natural dopamine stores.

The healthy way, the path of greater resistance, is diet and exercise. When I heard "diet and exercise" from my doctor I immediately used my disability as an excuse, not a reason. The difference being that my disability, and to a large extent my ignorance and laziness, were the reasons for my health, but I was using it as an excuse to pop a pill, watch a movie, and not go to the gym. The difference between a reason and an excuse is quite simply the willingness to do the work to get better, to maintain a healthy lifestyle. Diet and exercise is not the path of least resistance, so we naturally look to Western Medicine to cure our pains rather than release our own body's healing properties.

Once I gained a bit of reason over my physical limitations, I found something that I could do. I became an open water marathon swimmer and am now swimming and eating for health. I'm no longer using my disability as an excuse, and outside of the core physical impairment am no longer disabled due to my efforts. I overcame a physical condition to find the best health of my life despite deficiencies in age, body makeup, and natural ability. My disability became the reason to get better. My pain has subsided without the need for medication, and my diet supports my activity goals in a healthy and balanced way. The only thing is, it's not the path of least resistance.

I also want to tie this into the diffusion of responsibility argument and consumerism arguments made above. This leads me to the question of personal responsibility, for we've fallen victim to societal flaws that deprive us of personal independence, power, and overall strength. We trade our long term health for purchased short term fixes all of the time for both convenience and comfort. Our societal need to take the easy way can be seen in medicine and diet to be sure, and those two are personal in nature, governing our long term independent health. Some people will say, "yeah but that's a more efficient way." Your savings account, physical and mental stability, and overall health will eventually disagree with you, as you spend more and more hours seeking out professional health providers. Paying others to help get you back on the road to personal wellness is not only expensive, but inefficient with money and time resources. Furthermore, you may not be fully invested in long term health changes and may just be paying for short term comfort. This will eventually lead to a decrease in your personal finances, and create time loss as you depend on service providers for personal care. This is time that may have been better spent in the gym, or in making that long overdue salad.

Societal flaw six:

We have made the assumption that the earth and all things on it belong to the human race, and this creates friction in the way of Yin and Yang. The truth of it is that humans and all life belong to Mother Earth. As we damage our earth, we damage ourselves. As are all things, we are rooted in mother earth, and without our roots we will not survive. We are best served in relation to ourselves and our independent balance when we seek to find oneness with the earth, as we are only a seed in the expanse of the history of mother-nature.

Therefore, the folly of the human race can be seen in how, as a race, we utilize natural resources. We use, but don't replenish. If this is a societal flaw, then there is high potential that it is also a personal flaw in all but those who intensely resist it. Humans have a duality with nature, yet we as a society are intent on building cities. We are consumers, not for the sake of need, but for the sake of want. In many cases this want leads to addiction due to weakness and a lack of understanding of our own nature. If we are to be balanced, we must get back to our relationship with nature itself. We are one with nature, not at odds with nature. With the significant changes to our environment looming upon us in the way of an increase in natural disasters and pandemics, our world is balancing in the way Yin/Yang requires, and will continue to do so upon our overconsumption.

This struggle is an internal one, first, that causes our external outcomes, and diffusion of responsibility is the cause. This responsibility starts with that of our own bodies and minds, and then can branch out to protect others and the world overall. Your ability to make a difference depends on your ability to understand your dependent relationship with nature. Nature is where you can most easily find balance and the understanding that does not align with the industrial complex of human overconsumption.

I do realize that I'm part of this concern as well, just writing this on a computer, printing it on paper, and selling it creates a ripple against the interests of nature, and one could argue it's also a narcissistic act. In the interest of protecting the human race and Mother Earth prior to our mutually ensured destructions, we must educate society. To be involved in this line of education is to change outcomes, and to place light in the way of the world.

Societal flaw seven:

Our society attempts to control the future actions of people through systematic shame and judgement. By maintaining a system of imprisonment and corporal punishment, the resulting societal rule based upon the precedent set by our judicial system is that it's acceptable to control and even kill other people. In this way society lacks leadership by example. This argument is not

54

to say that crime should be tolerated, the argument is that we should celebrate redemption and subsequent forgiveness. There is little room for forgiveness within our current justice system. Even upon release, the individual's ability to earn and provide is hampered, leading to a greater chance of repeat offense. Worse yet, our justice system is disproportionately levied against minorities and the disadvantaged through fear, and Us vs Them mentalities.

Societal flaw eight:

We place individual labels on people or groups through a lens of fear. This creates an Us vs Them mindset and a relationship that is inevitably at odds for a sense of survival or for resources. For the purpose of the Empath, society, and (by force) this book, we have labeled people Narcissists (people who cause me pain). I've taken time to draw a picture that shows that we are all Narcissists.

I've noticed a trend of Empaths being in relationships with narcissistic individuals, and this trend points to a love expectation; however, in the end the other person does not reciprocate, and rather responds with manipulation, and disappointment matched with heartache is now upon the Empath. This may result in retreat from society due to distrust. It is important to not associate with manipulative individuals. It is important to use the skills provided throughout the remainder of this book to know of these individuals, and your natural tendencies toward them.

An Empath's greatest strength is in their heart and ability to heal others. Although those people who damage us seem a worthy cause, unless they are on a path of healing and self-improvement their need to manipulate you and all situations will result in personal devastation. Until you are strong enough, it is recommended to set boundaries with these people and begin a no contact policy. In the case that you are required to have this person in your life due to, for instance, having a child together, there are a couple of routes that you can take. Here is a list of ideas; these can apply well to individuals in abusive relationships.

1. Set boundaries to a text only relationship.

2. Obtain a mediator that works as a go between so that there is no direct contact.

3. Take no opinions that they are able to disagree with.

4. Compliment them to keep them placid, but maintain the boundaries so that you may live your own life.

5. Don't take the bait; if you are confronted, observe them, but limit your reactions. Taking the bait may create an argument, and that's what they need in order to obtain power over you.

6. Appear disinteresting; don't be dramatic. Be boring in their eyes so that they feel no need to engage with you.

7. Grow stronger and develop your sense of self. Begin a healthy relationship with yourself and others. Manipulative people generally know when they can't win, and with more strength and healthy relationships this will become apparent.

8. Leave the situation if you can. You are better and stronger than them, even if not in this moment. By leaving, you will be.

9. Send them positivity when they are not around you. Most likely they cannot source their good feelings, so if they feel better when away, they will be more inclined to stay away.

The state of our general society is out of balance going all the way back to the discussion posed in Societal flaw one. Your largest priority should be to find love for yourself, and back it with an internal and external voice, for one pebble creates a large ripple. Picking up the emotions of another is a natural tendency for an Empath, as we intend to help the other person by taking it off of them, but we are unable to be grounding blocks for the entire world and maintain our own mental health at the same time. This practice speaks to your enormously large heart and your love for others, but will damage you over time. Once you are in a good place you can choose to make these connections, but in the meantime, it's an unnecessary hardship.

It's also notable that you are not responsible for the well-being of the other person. If they choose to be in the place they are, and you try to take some of that off of them absorbing it into your being, they will simply replace what you took since they will feel emptiness without it. People are always filling emotional holes, and they are ultimately unfillable. Wrongs will always haunt, but our power over them is not in filling an unfillable hole, it's in making peace with its existence and learning how to not fall in. Projecting our want for self-love onto others (the people we attract naturally) can be devastating, and we are often attracted to doing so due to our own unfillable holes. We have a tendency as Empaths to think, "If I love them and they are happy, they in turn will love me, and I will then be happy." There is a line between internal and external love. That which comes from within provides balance, longevity, and inspiration to all that you do. That which comes externally can support, but ultimately may not sustain your expectations, leaving you disappointed in the other individual and ending in resentment.

US VS THEM

We have evolved in groups as a way of survival. Within our current society, if we feel alone or without a group this can cause great distress. If we are accepted by a group, it's part of our nature to protect that bond and compete for resources, which can lead to an Us vs Them mentality. This is the case with all major business/sports groups and teams. We protect our house, sometimes at all costs and leading to violence against Them. But if we pause, we take a moment to understand They are just like Us, defending their territory and competing for resources.

In a world of plenty, given resources are available, why do we have such imbalance with greater than 40% of our monetary resources being owned by less than 1% of the world population? Us vs Them and accumulation through Greed. These individuals are generally in The Dark or there would be no need to amass such personal possessions. There are great exceptions, and charitable individuals' giving on enormous scale, and those examples are of The Light. To break this conflict, all people should make an effort to have compassion for all those unlike you every day.

Take time today and pay attention to every time you label someone as unlike you. This makes that person in your mind a Them, not an Us. It could be the obvious: sex, race, religion, but it could also be more subtle as social class, work position, clothing style, hair color, or if they eat salad or pasta for lunch. What you'll begin to notice is that Them is really Us. Don't just stop at the human race and all of our differences, continue that thought to all living things and Mother Nature herself, because there is no Them, it's only Us. We came up together, and in the situation that we go down we will do so together, regardless of social class or species.

You, an Empath, know in your heart that there is no Us vs Them. There is just Us, and you, with your gift, don't feel the world in Us vs Them, you just feel the world. I will qualify this a bit because you feel the consequences of Us vs Them society every day. You feel the hate, the competition, the betrayal, the distrust, the poverty, the death, and the anguish throughout the world, you feel all of the societal downfalls of Us vs Them. This is enough to make you want to protect yourself, and no one, most of all me, blames you for this. But I love you too much to see you live a half-life or suffer death through depression like I did.

TRAUMATIC EVENTS

"Maintaining order rather than correcting disorder is the ultimate principle of wisdom."

-Nei Jing – Second Century BC

Accumulative Society lacks a collective experience, and this ignorance often overrides individual experience. You may have experienced this backwards. As the overall society lacks the collective knowingness of an Empath, there is a fallback tendency to resort to force for the resolution of all challenges. This will not change until a time where knowingness and connection to the collective life experience result in trust, formulating peace.

At the bottom of the human existence is depression accompanied by a feeling of hopelessness. This is met with a certain apathy towards change or effort, and the energy of the body is drained. People who are experiencing this are in a state of survival, and this can cause fear with overbearing anger. People who are simply surviving are not able to dream, and without a dream there feels as if there is no purpose. Those in this cycle often resent others who are functioning just highly enough that envy builds and plans of revenge find action. This action is meant to terrorize and disrupt the viewed success.

As a timely expansion to Societal Flaw one, violence stemming from anger is the predominant feeling that is expressed within our society. This is due to individuals feeling backed into a corner and a need to engage their fight or flight mechanism. Since they often feel trapped, the default response is fight. Their senses are often clouded by anger, and they either lash out or face a personal truth. Often, this personal truth or perceived threat appears too painful to face, so they lash out at others and place blame, harming others in the process. If you can see through all of the harm done, this is most commonly a cry for help, but the individual will often not admit to it being anger, a need for help, or personal truth, but will cover it up with pride through endless justification.

Concerning the wellbeing of an Empath, traumatic events are best resolved through an outpouring of love. If you are in a loving place toward the victims and are in a place to reach the families, even if reaching out to only one of a multitude of people, you will find a sense of personal peace. Reaching out and supporting others helps to balance the oneness within. Tragedy may already have happened, but it's the public's attitude in the wake of that tragedy that denotes peace both internally and externally. Media can be a big concern here, because often the media does not focus on the support of the victims. The media focuses on prolonging the pain through following the investigation, which, ultimately, acts as a glorification of it. This rarely is overshadowed by the outpouring of love and support for the victims.

The painful truth about traumatic events is that we cannot control the actions of others. Furthermore, it's the children of violence that become the perpetrators of violence because they were not adequately provided with knowledge of love, and society in general has not breached the barrier of a peaceful and loving society. It can also be said that we've lost the village aspect of raising children due to fear. We live more and more in small family groups behind closed doors. In every way, we create our own problems through apathy, fear, inaction, and lack of leadership. If all could realize the teachings of self-love, then these systems would simply fade away and the human collective would find peace.

The following is a poem I wrote after one of the many senseless mass shootings. It illuminates my feeling of being cornered by my Empathic tendencies. I wanted to share it, as days like these are always difficult.

Empath to Self Love

The decline of sensibility,

entropy my only governing entity,

to curl, to cry.

Sleep till goodbye, nothing left to give,

further receipt, only pain replies.

Death reinforces choice to live,

threatens resolve. Give.

Broad-based society,

pain's emotional wire, tired,

sanity's sill, sunshine's given all, but is eclipsed, retired.

Can't shut off, can't give in!

Mind, don't leave me, don't pass, Begin!

No, pause…. pain's emotional wire.

No! Pause!

To curl, to cry, no pause, please pause, no more death, no more die.

I choose not to feel this way, but don't have a vote.

Empathies rule: Always side with the one that doesn't have a vote.

Why does that have to be me? Entropy, empathy, defined.

Tortured we are, more the benefit others,

the worse they make us feel.

Always side with the one that doesn't have a vote.

Love thyself, too, the only remaining reveal.

THE SCIENCE

Now that we understand the society that we are born into, let's lay a foundation of the science that can bridge us to a new life.

THE HUMAN BRAIN AND OUR EVOLUTION

The human brain has not been able to keep up with our rate of evolution. In a very short time, our previous concerns such as food, shelter, and tribe have been morphed into a large societal complex that holds little call for the survival instincts still ingrained in our brain. This information is extremely helpful to you as an Empath. Although not proven in this context, I theorize that Empaths have a more highly developed limbic area of the brain. Upon receiving a stimulus, the limbic area is the first stop along the pathway of personal analysis of the information received. The limbic area is where your emotions are housed, it is also me the first stop on the empathic connection line. The limbic area is responsible for your Fight or Flight response, along with your emotional wellbeing, including joy, sadness, and a host of potentially irrational responses. Our ancestors used this for survival, reacting to stimuli that may have caused them to be eaten by a predator. It's built for, "Oh no, I'm being attacked by a saber tooth tiger!" which causes us to raise our spear, and is not necessarily built for, "That guy cut me off!" which results in road rage. The limbic area of our brain doesn't apply reason, so it does not know the difference.

We always process our emotions first, and this has purpose. It's kept us alive, giving us the ability to defend ourselves against threats to our wellbeing. Furthermore, it's how we perceive our world. Emotions shape how we frame our thoughts and feelings about everything we interact with.

We make this more challenging as we have a natural need to be right, we want our intuition to be correct, because we rely on it so heavily. Think about it in terms of that gut feeling you have about the person you met in the bar. You knew before they even spoke to you that they were not someone you wanted to hang out with. It could be the exact opposite too, the person that you ended up dating for a long time; marriage and children follow because it just clicked, and you knew that this was "love at first sight."

We have a built-in radar for these things, and we want it to be right, so much so that we can create the outcome, even if it's dangerous, unhealthy, and/or harmful to us. When we do reinforce these feelings, we often justify them endlessly as pride and further our residence in The Dark.

It is also notable that the limbic area of your brain does not process any language, so it only processes raw feeling and governs immediate threat reaction. As Empaths we are also processing the vibrations of the wellbeing of society. This is where Empaths often get stuck, but this does us no good. Slowing this process down helps us to engage our mental processing centers and keeps us from responding in potentially regrettable ways.

Next in the processing line of our neural network is the Neo-Cortex, and that is where we need to be to make sense of all of the emotions that we are processing. The Neo-Cortex is responsible for analyzing the stimulus, verbalizing it so that it may be explained internally and externally, and formulating a logical response. Due to our immense processing power, both processes combined take less than a second; however, when we analyze the information provided, its initial thought is always clouded with our sense of emotion towards it.

A good sign that we are working with our limbic area is that we will speak in statements of absolutes: "I (He, She) never," or "I always." These are emotionally driven statements that, inside of our feelings, are always right.

We even go so far as to defend them if questioned, and at times will make them come true in the future just to prove a point, regardless of our own personal loss in the process. The strategy to avoid responding with emotion prior to reason is to slow the process and engage our Neo-Cortex. There are many ways to do this, including but not limited to:

1. Collect factual information about your surroundings.

2. Count backwards from five to one.

3. Draft an emotional response, and then work to edit it without sending the message to anyone.

4. Take time to consider if their harm to you is intentional.

5. Name the emotion – Don't use "Good or Bad," call it what it is.

6. Grounding (concentrating on something that enlightens your senses and provides focus).

7. Muscle Testing concerning the situation.

These suggestions all slow the process and engage logic over our emotional programming.

IMAGINATION

The human and the squirrel share the same hard-wiring. The trouble is, our minds are far more complex and can create scenarios far more efficiently than a squirrel. We both attempt to separate ourselves from danger. We both attempt to maintain pleasure and escape pain. We both seek out stability, safety, and sustenance. Humans simply have the processing power to create problems, where a squirrel is more likely to go on their merry way to the next opportunity and learn through more experience. Unlike the squirrel, we do far more than remember. We recite, replay, block out, black out, drink and drug away, and make up reasons why we should feel a certain way.

We have the intellect to find more and more creative ways to traumatize or sedate ourselves in the name of not dealing with our own mind. In summary, we can choose to stop living for any number of reasons, shunning more opportunity due to something that our mind labeled as negative. So, if the mind focusing on negativity is the challenge, then the mind focusing on the positive is the solution.

I often tell my own children, "Don't get creative." In one light, this can be seen as incredibly hypocritical because I myself am a very creative individual. Imagination creates all of the human good and all of the human bad. The good parts of human creativity produce art, music, charity. In another light, the bad parts of human creativity create suicide, promiscuous relationships, destruction, recreational drugs, and war. The bad parts are what I'm referring to when I tell my children to not get creative, and it's generally right before something gets broken or someone gets hurt.

We are constantly spinning the story of our lives and have more than enough aptitude to do so. Furthermore, the human race is wired for survival, so we are looking for risks and threats to analyze. This programs us to look for the negative. To truly thrive, we must challenge ourselves to stay mentally active. This bridges the gap, for without stimulation we will imagine. Imagining positively and in a creative light allows for the creation of the positives in society. To live in the moment is to live a life of beauty, compassion, and forgiveness. Imagining in a negative light allows for the creation of the negatives in society. Trouble starts up when we don't have actual threats to analyze and begin instead to imagine them. To take this a bit further, the result is anxiety, which I define as a physical reaction to the imagined worst-case scenario. Imagination is either the solution or the problem, it just depends on which side of that coin you choose to reside.

Don't react to your reactions, that way you can stop your mind from getting creative with a situation. Don't imagine the worst-case scenario, because you'll make it come true, and that may cost you years of healthy living. When my grandfather (childhood Dad) passed away in my early teens, I had no concept of how to grieve. I created an expectation based on all of the imagined pain that I thought a person should feel, and held myself in that torment through a seven-year depression full of alcohol abuse. I made my imagined problem come true to the point of unlikely escape. Then I woke up one day and realized that I could no longer mourn and be stuck in that grief. I released him, and this was the first day of my life as I know it.

The mind is the opportunity. Consider if I would not have reacted with an imagined way to grieve. There would have been a period of pain while trying to figure it out, but if I'd released that pain within a day or a week, or even a month, I still would have lived a far healthier lifestyle, and could probably remember or have felt far more of the next seven years. What I learned is: living in the past or an imagined future is not living at all, it's dying. Living is to make the best of this moment, and let the positivity of each of those moments stack on top of each other to create a beautiful life. If you do this consistently the internal lights will all turn on, leaving The Dark behind. This may also create a beautiful legacy. Being remembered as the person everyone felt better around is a benefit of being an Empath. Being that person without sacrificing the self is the point of being kind and compassionate to yourself, building the strength to walk through the fire of your life, and loving those around you.

I think of this in Bricks and Balloons. I'll sometimes utter to myself: "You are when you are." Balloons that we hold in the future are of the thought, "when I get this, I'll be happy." Bricks that chain us to the past are, "when this happened, I was hurt, so I will not forgive or let go, and can no longer be happy." Those balloons in the future can turn to lead and hold us down from greater aspirations, not allowing us realistic vision to carve out a path to success. Furthermore, if/when we achieve them, we often find that they did not make us happy, and we just replace them with something else to occupy our minds. There will always be another balloon because balloons align with desire.

The bricks become our graves, causing us to obsess over things we no longer have control over. Bricks often align with guilt and weigh us down, anchoring us in the past. As such, forgiveness is the way to release ourselves from the anguish of the past. The phrase, "You are when you are" is speaking about becoming as close to real time as possible in your day to day life, and not seeking out an imagined future or being haunted by the past or things outside of our scope of immediate control. If we are to be truly well, then now is the time to be well, because now is the time we have direct and meaningful control over our actions. A good summary phrase I say to myself and others on occasion is, "At the end of the day, the only person you need impress is yourself." This provides personal freedom, as it's dismissive of the opinions, and judgement of others. For some people, this can be getting out of bed and taking a shower. In practice and over time this turns into courage, freedom, and self-compassion. Every day, even every waking moment, is a choice; choose positivity, and soon enough it will become a lifestyle of acceptance and love.

Calibrate where you were with where you want to be, and you'll find your present. This is your center, and your understanding of who you are in this moment. Many times, it's the things in our past that just keep dragging us backwards. Once you are confident in your present there's a moment when you need to denounce your demons. Let it be known in no uncertain terms that you are in control, and cannot be beaten. We are human, and therefore fallible; if we do not denounce our demons and fight our inherent flaws we will again fall. This is a daily reckoning, but in time will be taken for granted, allowing your breadth of leadership to find the breath to assist others.

Compassion in the form of forgiveness for one's self is the key to personal evolution. The mistakes of the past are to be left in the past - remembered, but not relived. Your real life is in the now; align with positivity and honesty to love yourself in this moment. Remember this moment, and recreate its relative mental space as necessary to frame the remainder of your days in light.

OUR SUBCONSCIOUS MIND

The old saying is that we use 10% of our mind. This has been proven false. The updated version is that we use 5% of our conscious mind and the remainder of our mental aptitude, nearly 95% is utilized subconsciously. We are constantly making subconscious decisions that shape our overall life. Even more importantly, we are constantly programing our subconscious mind with code/language denoting future actions. I use the term code because, much like in computer programing, we are inputting language into our database that helps us make future decisions. Most of the language is absorbed during our youth, between birth and age six, when we are observing our parents. This is when our Hard Line becomes set, and much of the time, despite our best efforts to resist, we subconsciously end up just like our parents through like choices.

Let's learn a bit about our subconscious mind. Throughout this conversation, please remember that we are constantly programing our subconscious, and even though we don't tune into it consciously we whole heartedly believe everything it says. Think of it this way, remember when you were young and learned to ride a bike. You had to master the thought of pedaling, and then steering, all while considering balance. This took a lot of conscious processing. Little by little, it got easier as you practiced and repeated the task. Through practice you were inputting code into your subconscious, and it was all filed away under riding a bike, and more importantly the emotions you had towards it. Then one day you got really good at it, and no longer had to think about the pedals, handlebars, balance, or any of the mechanics that were once top of mind. Today, even if you haven't ridden in years, you could get back on a bike and go for a ride because the coding for this activity is embedded and the language familiar. This is a singular, and relatively harmless, example of the mechanics of how we utilize our subconscious.

So, you've gotten really good at riding your bike. You are so good that you no longer need to use your handlebars to steer all of the time. You are proud of this, and revel in the feeling of exhilaration when you let go, sit tall, engage your pedals, and feel the wind in your hair. Every once in a while, you wobble, and you even fall sometimes, but it seems worth it. Then another person comes along and tells you, "It's dangerous!" (instilling fear), and, "You are not good enough at riding a bike to manage riding without handlebars." We read this feedback with our emotions first, and start writing code to our subconscious. Our subconscious is a manual processer of code, it reads what you provide it, and, as discussed, we process our emotions first, so every bit of code written into your subconscious has an emotion tagged to it. What's worse, when we are making decisions based on subconscious thought, it's that emotional tag that gets referenced first. Furthermore, our subconscious doesn't code the whole story; like language, it originates a notes version of the full narrative, and then files it away.

In this situation the subconscious would code the fear that was given us. This would first be realized in the form of riding a bike without handlebars, but may later in life may stop you from trying sky diving because of an innate fear of falling that you can't even track back to this conversation. The other piece of this that you may code would be, "You are not good enough." We have a tendency to hold onto words like these. Although the original message was intended to protect you, our minds don't always retain the context of the information; rather, we subconsciously generalize its gist to all factors in life based on emotion. If you felt fear, embarrassment, or shame due to the situation, all like situations will refer subconsciously to this memory or memories like it. The original message becomes a shadow of the intended message.

Our subconscious makes 95% of our decisions, so it's valuable to gain some level of reason with it. As we are prone to focus on the negative, we very well take "You're not good enough" out of this conversation. We may endlessly internalize this, and although our no-handlebar bike-riding days are long gone and behind us, this potential dating experience with a fascinating person feels exciting and invigorating, like riding that bike without using handlebars, and instead of embracing it, we freeze and think, "I'm not good enough." Sadly, we hardly remember the original circumstance; we don't remember the words spoken, but we subconsciously reference the emotional tag and are instantly flooded with a belief system that is hard to escape. The self-coded subconscious reciprocates the language we provided it as truth, and, sadly, we believe it with all of our heart, because it originates internally.

These small slights, even if meaningless to us in the moment, can manifest into large concerns later in life. Within the context of this example, if we wanted to take on a new task, we may think twice because ingrained in our subconscious is a figment of the original emotionally tagged language that places fear, and tells us learning something new isn't worth it. This type of feedback cycle can happen hundreds if not thousands of times within childhood to protect you or temper your expectations. Disappointment and a certain amount of damage to your confidence are often immediate and long term byproducts. It's the reaction to the emotions that codes to our subconscious that haunts us later.

Decades later, we may be faced with a job opportunity, dating situation, or public speaking opportunity, and in place of confidence we freeze or self-destruct for lack of confidence at a subconscious level. At times, we even externalize our internal dialogue, sabotaging our opportunity so that we reinforce our subconscious belief and prove ourselves correct. If you truly believe "I'm not good enough," then you may as well be correct, right? This does us no good, it's time to stop the cycle, and even if we've missed opportunities in the past, today is a new day and we can recode our subconscious with new love language.

Remember going through the Traits of an Empath? Remember that I duplicated Genius? This is why; I wanted to subconsciously encode that Genius is the predominant factor of being an Empath. I wanted to do that above all others because we do utilize our whole intelligence. Empaths are Genius! Now let's learn to gain some level of conscious control over our subconscious.

THE EXPECTATIONS OF CHILDHOOD

I want to share a bit of a personal story here. I grew up in Western Nebraska where my Grandfather managed an acreage, and within it, horses. This acreage was lined with an electric fence. As a child you touch things, and this creates knowledge. When you touch an electric fence without knowledge it quickly provides shock as a learning opportunity, and that shock instils fear. My subconscious mind assigned that same fear tag to many curiosities and obstacles I would face going forward. It did this without my conscious knowledge, and it wasn't until decades later that I realized the original electric fence in my life still contained me. I mentally fenced myself inside that original electric fence, along with a host of relatable experiences that wrote to my subconscious language. One could argue that this was out of protection, but one could also argue that it introduced self-limiting factors, and took away my power of discovery. Much of my story is written about my struggle to reclaim this power, the ability to stand on my own and cut through my mental electric fences. I now liken this path to buying a pair of insulated wire cutters. With these in my toolbox, I eventually breached that first electric fence and others like it. I was able to expand my thinking, and subsequently my world.

Understanding the expectations of childhood is important to us now, so that we can draw a line between our past and present. The expectations that we conform to and that we form as assumptions of the world as children can have long-lasting effects throughout our adulthood. There should be a realistic checkpoint to this somewhere in our early adulthood, but as emotions fly around, we don't slow down to realize:

1. As a child, you lacked choice about important things such as living location, family, shelter, food, and responsibility.

2. As a child, you were almost always at the low point of the power dynamic of the family/societal unit.

3. As a child, you were not fully responsible for your own protection.

4. As a child, you observed your environment as your primary source of learning.

5. As a child, you lacked resources to effect substantial change in your life.

6. As a child, you followed an enforced set of rules, founded upon the experience of others.

Now:

1. As an adult, you have more power over the direction and scope of your life.

2. As an adult, the differences in the power perspective in your relationships are minimal.

3. As an adult, you are the primary individual who is responsible for your self-protection.

4. As an adult, you have endless opportunities to self-educate.

5. As an adult, you have far more resources and control over resources than you had in your childhood.

6. As an adult, you can leverage learnings to take on more challenges and manage your subconscious language through choice.

It is understandable that the expectations you set in your childhood would have far reaching consequences in adulthood - put me in that boat.

With that said, it's far more reasonable now than it was then for you to leave the past in the past. Now you can make changes and decisions that will benefit you in the future. Many people don't graduate from childhood expectations, despite aging into a system that rewards work, choice, and education. The same level of graduation may be applied to being an Empath. Being in The Dark makes being an Empath a daily battle, but there is a progression, and if you can find courage in this, you may open the door to self-love. This is a state where your gifts are tangible to yourself and others, and your light becomes bright with leadership. It works full circle, and you'll finally gain control over the gift we are all born with.

EMPATHIC CHILDREN

To children, knowing they are tapped into a bigger system of communication is automatic. It's common to think that empathy is something that only a few of us have, even though we all create vibrations. Baby Vibe is my term for a magical time - between birth and when the language centers in toddlers begin to develop - where our littles ones are all Empathic. You may notice that they *see* you; they know who can communicate on their level, so they will seek you out. I love speaking with the little ones that don't yet have language. They are pure and honest, and their strength is housed in the fragility of infant skin. They will always turn and look, often smile, and wave, and in some cases physically reach out. As your skills grow, so will their interaction with you. Their precious eyes and aura can feel your light, and that creates an instant bond.

It saddens me, but this turns and begins to shut off when they begin learning language. It's like the brain begins to get rid of the old method of communication which is universal and pure in favor of the new. It's terrible, but for many children it's lost forever, inaccessibly buried in the background of their subconscious. For others, the shut off is temporary, and some of us hold on. Maybe it's part of our hard wiring, innate to the point where we cannot shut it off.

Our children become torn between two worlds. Some call this time the terrible twos. From my experience as a parent, I think three is the hardest age for our littles and I sympathize with them. They are learning at an amazing rate, but language is replacing their birth communication method. This puts them in a tricky spot, and much of the time this is when their night terrors and tantrums begin. As their social circles expand, they can feel others, but are unable to fully reason pain, and are now torn between their feelings and a language they don't yet grasp. They are trying to reason someone else's cry for help without the necessary language to do so. This creates internal torment, and as parents, the best we can do is try to shield them from it by boosting our Empathic communication with them. It's a lot to expect of a child who is doing everything they can to integrate into society, so be patient at this time.

From an enlightenment perspective, in my experience, all babies begin in an enlightened state, but then revert to learning language and societal norms. It is up to the individual to maintain or get back to the prior state, and it's within each of us to do so in adulthood. In the meantime, we have limited control, so it's important as parents to realize that if you are Empathic, and it is something you are in tune with, your child most likely will be too. Empathic abilities have been traced to genetics. The point is, being Empathic and enlightened is our birthright, a direct line through the gift of knowing, and it's up to the parent to protect it as your children integrate into society.

Society teaches us how to feel, and worse yet, how to hide our feelings, creating guilt, shame, and sadness, for we are often not taught productive ways of ridding ourselves of negativity. Even something as innocent as a Mother telling her child to not be afraid of the storm outside places a perspective of fear on the child concerning storms. In other words, there's no right way to raise a child; we can only do our best through love, reinforcing their personal light. Boost their personal signals, and teach them so that they don't shut off. It's a lot to handle, and a lot to expect, but if you are reading this, you most likely know what it's like to try and figure it out on your own years later.

PERSONALITY WALLS

A warning about walls: Walls, over time, become destructive to the self, as we begin to distrust all things outside of the wall. When this happens, I call it a Personality Wall. As we lock ourselves in, we lose perspective, and our imaginations make it difficult to get back out. Yes, public places, cities, and sometimes your very own home become overwhelming with thoughts, but as you address them, you reclaim your power. Practice makes one sane, but building walls, or the attempt at building walls, creates anxiety when they don't work or begin coming down.

The reason Personality Walls exist is to block others out. The other way to see that is that you are walling off the Empathic you. As you try to imprison the thoughts you also imprison the Empath inside. You're locking away your heart, compassion, and sensitivity along with it. This, at the very least, is painful and leads to a change in decisions, which leads to a change in behaviors, which leads to a change of personality. As all of the beautiful pieces of you that are associated with your heart become locked away, it's only logical that you feel lost and in a state of emotional torment. We need to understand that this is our natural tendency. If we hurt, then we try to distance ourselves from that pain.

Personality Walls, above all, are a self-created fire in your life that you must walk through. You cannot wall yourself off and still truly live, trust, and love. This starts with you, and as all things that start, those things also must end. I urge you to let your walls softly crumble over time. They come down because we are meant to be soft, and walls are the Yang to our natural Yin. We are meant to be compassionate, and being hard and rigid, which is what our walls require, is fearful and exhausting. It's Empathic kryptonite, and we feed it to ourselves out of a lack of understanding.

Telling you that they need to come down now would be incredibly hypocritical, so I won't dare do that. Instead, place some soft places to land on each side of them so that when they crumble you won't be in pain and trying to rebuild. Rebuilding walls is time and energy wasted. Soft landings allow you the freedom to experience, trust, and forgive. Just like your walls need a soft place to land, so do the thoughts that built them. The thoughts and decisions in relation to your walls are thoughts that were not addressed. In place of walking through the fire to address those imposing thoughts, you imprisoned a piece yourself in the same prison cell. As that wall comes down, those thoughts may escape too. Addressing each one compassionately gives you power over them, and takes the power they once had away. We will discuss strategies at great length in the solution driven sections of this book. For now, simply know that Personality Walls only retain the energy that you expend building and maintaining them, and by repurposing that energy into self-compassion, you will gain freedom from them.

PEPTIDES, KIDNEY, SPIRIT, MEMORY

We are Empathic partly because the point at where the brain ends and the body begins is not readily identifiable. The nerves emanating from our spine blend into our organs. In addition, white blood cells communicate and operate together with collective memory to dispose of invading cells. Furthermore, blood can be considered connective tissue due to its uses of plasma. Thus, the body is the brain, and the brain is the body. To further this argument, in Chinese Medicine the water in your body is managed by the kidneys, and the kidneys operate as a memory center. Interestingly, in both Chinese and Western Medicine, kidney failure and mental degradation are linked. As discussed previously, the heart has memory and also generates Qi, or the spirit, which is then amplified and protected by the pericardium. The blood carries the Qi, and connects all of the organs together. There is no separation, there is only a whole that is part of the greater whole.

Within the body are hormones which operate as neurotransmitters and make up part of the communication system within our bodies. The most prominent point is that feelings, focus, and attitudes are addictive, and these feelings are conducted by hormones. The easiest example of attitude addiction to cite is an adrenaline junky, unpredictable and engaging in risky behavior. They require constant input that creates a fear response, leading to the body fueling with adrenaline. This fear creates an addictive environment within the body, and to the outside world the individual becomes angry and aggressive. The bigger picture is that the body responds with adrenaline to thoughts of negativity, creating immediate weakness. This adrenaline is also acidic, and over time damages the body.

The counter-perspective establishes that the body responds to challenge and positivity with endorphins. This outlook creates immediate strength. Endorphins, dopamine, serotonin have a calming effect on the organs and the mind. The law of physics applies beautifully here, "every action has an equal and opposite reaction." Your thoughts create a downline effect within the body because replicated cells seek out the conditions under which they were created. They will continually crave their originating chemical makeup of neurotransmitters, steroids, and peptides.

Peptides are created within the brain by the hypothalamus to provide communication channels to the rest of the body. If you feel happy, you produce happy peptides. If you feel sad, angry, apathetic, etc., you produce like peptides and slowly program your body to crave those emotions. If enough of these are created you reach a tipping point, physically becoming what you think. At that point, depression programs more depression, just as joy programs more joy. What's more, your immune system, cell structures, and world view are tied. It takes time to build it either way. You can't be made negative or positive overnight, but make no mistake, you are programing your body to seek out and crave the type of peptide that you were producing in that moment.

While you are thinking, feeling, and producing peptides, your body is replicating cells. We replicate a new blood supply every two months, and your blood feeds every cell in your body. Concerning the rest of your body, every cell is replaced every two years. Each cell created is not necessarily a carbon copy of its predecessor, as it is formed around the constantly changing communication system. This communication system is considered an ongoing and updating memory center of the body that is outside of the scope of the brain.

Adrenalin – Fight or Flight, Anger

Cortisol – The Stress Hormone

Dopamine – Calm/Impulse Control

Histamine – The Irritant - associated with the liver - allergies, rashes, hives, bites.

Oxytocin – The Love Hormone

Serotonin – The Happy Hormone

The prevailing question is: Why not build a positive, healthy body that can withstand the challenges that life will give? Within every struggle, there is an opportunity to help yourself grow stronger within the process. The point is, you can program your body to crave depression, fear, anger, or resentment, just like you can program your body to crave happiness, elation, peace, and joy. The choice is literally yours, as you are the only one in charge of what's taking place in your mind. The choice to view things as positive or negative has vast effects on your immune system, digestion, mental well-being, and longevity. Positivity (endorphins) leads to wellness. Negativity (adrenaline/acidity) leads to illness and pain (inflammation). You are creating this pain through your thoughts and your perspective toward the circumstances of your life. This is how depression and stress cause fatalities; the heart and immune system can only take so much.

Now, the challenge is to respond to this predicament presented by your body with a positive frame of mind , free of worry and stress. To do this will send healing energy through the system. As our blood supply creates a new generation every two months, just imagine the benefit to your entire body when the healing peptides of a positive mind frame turn the corner, tip the scales, and take hold. Western Medicine likes to call dramatic healing of the human condition a miracle, but in reality, it's just the body healing itself through a positive perspective upon adversity. In many cases, this is brought on by a near death experience and subsequent enlightenment. In other cases, this is brought on by a belief system. Either way, the body is responding to a positive stream of consciousness that derives healing benefits.

Just as athletes change their bodies through exercise, you can work out with a positive attitude to change your physical state. The combination of these factors working through steroids, hormones, and peptides produced by the body can remove pain and create health that can change a life.

EPIGENETICS – DNA AND THE SCIENTIFIC EXPLANATION BEHIND EVOLUTIONARY BEHAVIORISM

To take this conversation about peptides and how we program our bodies a bit further, let's talk about Epigenetics. The brain is mysterious; the progression of consciousness is inherited. That is to say, truth will breed more truth, and falsehood will breed more falsehood. This may be a function of teaching, but there is a genetic factor to consider. It has been found that through our activities, diet, exercise, stresses, and trauma, we can change how our DNA functions, or how it expresses itself at a cellular level. This expression is not a manipulation of the DNA itself, but rather how each independent cell functions (opens and closes).

Events over the course of your life can change the expression of your genes. These can then be passed down generationally. This could be a lifestyle choice or a behavior of a Father being inherited by a daughter, and then passed down again to a son. I refer to this commonly as a Hard Line or inherited behavior. These are incredibly difficult to break, but may explain why being Empathic is inherited. Factors in a life that can cause such a change include stress, famine, diet, medications, even surgical procedures. Traits that have been researched include cancer, blood disorders, lung disorders, and mental disorders. To change these factors is both simple and difficult. Simple, as we have the ability to choose our future lifestyle. Difficult, in the fact that our current lifestyle and related risk factors may be hard-wired into our DNA.

Studies have found that an individual can change how their DNA expresses through reduction of stress, diet (nutrition), and exercise as well as a support system influencing changed behaviors. This is true at a cellular level, but also aligns with the peptide discussion above. As an Empath, I'm interested in this because DNA is extremely reactive. Even when removed from the body and kept in a separate location, DNA reacts to the moods and feelings of the individual to whom it belongs. It will relax its structure with thoughts of love, and tighten its structure with thoughts of anger. This is proof that your attitude and mood actually interact with and can change your DNA.

DNA also interacts with the light around it. I think this is telling, as we create light within us that is tied to the concept of Qi. It's been shown that every cell in the body is sensitive to electromagnetic waves. Each cell transmits and receives vibrational frequencies and emits light. When our bodies are failing, we actually leak light, primarily from our fingertips and toes. When strong and vibrant, we retain light. Additionally, foundational to the makeup of our physiology, it's been shown that our reactions and thoughts can change the structure of the water in your body. What we think truly does impact our wellbeing on a physiological level. This is why stress is said to be as a silent killer.

MERIDIANS

Think about Chinese Medicine less in terms of science and more in terms of experience spooled up over centuries. Please have no expectation that your Western Medicine-based understanding of the organ networks will align with how Chinese Medicine views them. Organs within Western Medicine share little responsibility or connection. Those same organs in Chinese Medicine share purpose through connection within the scope of meridians and the body's welfare. The Chinese organ networks are based on Embryology and the lines drawn during our earliest development. The resulting medicine is based on the movement of Qi, the Spirit, and Yin/Yang.

Fascia in Western Medicine is seen as the stuff your organs and muscles are wrapped in to hold them in place, while fascia in Chinese Medicine is seen as the electrical conductor of the organ networks, and the conjoining factor within the embryological spaces of expanse in your body. Fascia makes up all of the meridian lines and combined points as manipulated through acupuncture that free up the organ networks to interact. If the body is out of balance, the body is then susceptible to illness as Qi becomes stagnant.

Acupuncture channels begin as embryological electrical conduits that allow the body to communicate and develop prior to birth. These channels are there prior to our brain and organs, and then expand and grow with the body, allowing the organs to communicate and conduct Qi throughout life. The points (acupuncture points) that we use to balance Qi are expansion points in our embryological development that work as flood gates, releasing and storing energy. As Qi always moves through the path of least resistance, if a gate is not functioning, we may experience stagnant Qi, like a dam blocking the natural flow of energy. This can lead to disfunction and radiating pain throughout the body. Pain is a messenger, a warning to get the body to change behavior. Through acupuncture, we may release this Qi to normal flow and function, restoring the natural energy movement of the body.

We are made to conduct energy. Bone is crystalline in structure, so it plays a part, but most of the energy within us travels between the fascia in our bodies. Fascia is primarily made up of collagen, which is an excellent conductor of energy because it's also crystalline in structure. Collagen not only conducts our body's energy, but creates energy too. In addition, fascia wraps every organ in our body, like a protective web of energy that allows communication with the rest of the body. Fascia also wraps our circulatory system. Our heart is wrapped in collagen, and this is called our pericardium. The pericardium is a conductor, but also works as an electrical shield protecting the heart and enabling our heart's ability to interact with other electrical fields. It also creates a resonance, like the body of a stringed instrument bellowing sound. The pericardium amplifies your heart's vibration, but it also captures the vibration of other hearts. You are connecting to those energy fields.

Acupuncture is a way of getting your Qi to restore function and ideal circulation to the body through the manipulation of meridians. Meridians are embryological expansion points on the body that correspond to the organ networks, promoting balance. They are made up of points that promote vitality within the network, and manipulating them can promote healthy movement of Qi. When Qi is in the wrong place or operating outside of the Golden mean it causes cancer, pain, inflammation, and further disfunction. Much of the time this is due to imbalance where the self-destruct nature of cells is altered or shut off completely, as is common in cancerous cells. It's also known that strong and balanced Qi can defeat cancer by regulating the system.

Acupuncture has been used to treat everything from addiction to mental well-being. I personally have cured nose bleeds, migraines, site pain, and night terrors within my immediate family. Acupuncture is not like a drug where the effects run their course over the next couple of hours and you need to take another pill. Taking drugs associated with Western Medicine, or also the street variety of them, can be an additional underlying cause for the illness. Acupuncture is a tool used in the rebalancing of the natural systems of the body, such as digestion and circulation, benefiting the movement of Qi. Once balance is obtained, it may then be maintained with few treatments as needed. It's not a prescription taken daily that may cause further imbalance and short-term gains. It's a meridian point and a needle, providing a non-invasive solution.

In the event you feel this could help you, its foundations run centuries back; it's built on trial and error on only living patients, and it's far removed from the microscope of Western Medicine. It promotes healing in a restorative way. It's also eloquent proof of the bioelectric fields that course through your body. As an Empath, you are not only in tune with your own energy (signatures/vibrations), but these energy fields are what you sense as an Empath, and are what you are reading in others. Emotions control the body; the body controls emotion. These bioelectrical fields are why you get overwhelming feelings from other people. Acupuncture is a way to balance that feedback channel and provide strength in balance through the adversity. Notably, Chiropractic care is also founded on the same principles of energy flow and balance. Chiropractic care and Acupuncture work wonders in tandem.

CHINESE MEDICINE ARCHETYPES

I want to include this section so that you may have a better understanding of Chinese Medicine and how this book, and you as an Empath, aligns with this as a foundational base of knowledge and human experience.

The Liver network is associated with the Wood Archetype. The Liver network is the ruler of the blood, as the blood holds the essence of Qi. As such, the liver is responsible for the distribution of resources to all parts of the body. A consistent flow of blood regulates the physical body and the mind, allowing steady movement and mental stability. When blood flow is limited, sickness can fall upon the individual. The related sub-organ in this network is the gallbladder, and this network also includes reproductive organs (not responsible for storage of the individual essence that is passed down to future generations).

The Heart network (Heart profile) is associated with the Fire Archetype. The Heart network is the ruler presiding over the whole of all systems. The heart pumps the blood throughout the system, encapsulating the essence of the spirit. In Chinese culture, the spirit is the accumulative life force known as Qi, and it is the heart's responsibility to maintain this. When the spirit resides in the body and is strong, all mental faculties are in order and the individual is bright, warm, *empathic*, and full of communication. When this network begins to fail, the spirit wanders or leaves the body. The related sub-organ is the small intestine.

The Spleen network is associated with the Earth Archetype. The Spleen network is responsible for producing resources for the body, much like a farmer harvesting the fields. This includes both moisture and energy, and the balance of those resources within the body. The related sub-organ is the stomach.

The Lung network is associated with the Metal Archetype. The Lung network is responsible for the receipt of air, and the skin is considered a third lung. The lung is responsible for maintaining vigor, clarity, and calm within the mind. This is where the phrase "take a deep breath" most likely originates. The lung, as it combines with the skin, is also responsible for the defense of the body and immunities. The related sub-organ is the large intestine.

The Kidney network is associated with the Water Archetype. The Kidney network is responsible for the storage of Qi, and the spirit's essence in case of times of shortage. The kidney's responsibility also includes the storage of the individual's essence for regeneration, including reproduction and the passing of knowledge (wisdom) formally obtained to the next in the line of succession. This assumes a responsibility in tandem with the Liver network for reproductive organs, but in the case of the Kidney network the responsibility is for the organs involved in storage of the individual essence, to be passed down to future generations. The related sub-organ is the bladder.

Our bodies need to balance energy to be well. Think of it this way, if you are always full of adrenaline, making your heart work at maximum capacity all the time, this will inevitably cause the heart to fail sooner than it would in a relaxed state. This is true for each organ in the body, including the brain, but more importantly for the body overall. I mention the brain specifically because Qi does not only provide physical support, but is also a conduit for emotional support. Our organs are always communicating with each other through electrical impulses, hormones, adrenaline, serotonin (kidney function), histamine levels (liver function), and insulin (pancreas function), which are all extremely important in mood and wellness. These hormones function as neurotransmitters, allowing all organs to communicate with the rest of the body in real time. In an ideal body, we are operating via the golden mean, because the golden mean allows efficient, unlimited growth and expansion to create and heal.

The process of relying on the body as an individual information system has not been completely lost, but has been hampered by Western Medicine. There is an entire group of people failed by the Western medical system who turn to the healing properties of aligning with higher power attractors, such as honesty, mentorship, and compassion, and who have escaped the clutches of self-doubt, addiction, pain, depression, and disability through the practice of positivity and the freedom caused by a change in attitude. Count me among them. First must come a true desire to change the circumstance of your life. I, for one, back you in your effort, as I have limitless love for you. Start small, build a foundation of truth, once that becomes easy it will feel simple to climb upon it to your greatest potential heights.

THE SOLUTION/ THE MIDDLE

KATABASIS

The Line between Life and Death - The Greeks had a word for the state where a person is neither dead or alive. That word is Katabasis, and the interesting thing is it applied exclusively to people whose hearts were beating and lungs working, but they lacked positivity. Katabasis means a descent (falling) of some sort. In Greek mythology, it's often a descent into the underworld (The Dark), and often it's a descent that was caused by ourselves due to a form of greed, dishonesty, and an ego that does not allow us to fail or be humble. It's the climb out of this hole that we will focus on next. We often fail to act, for we simply don't know any better, and it's not until we hit rock bottom that we find the courage to make a change. The point is, if you don't like the way that your life is turning out, then you must begin making different choices. For those functioning in a continued state of Katabasis, we must claw our way out of the self-dug hole one decision at a time in spite of our imagination, negative focus, and subconscious language.

I call the following strategies the middle because in the David R Hawkins scale there's nothing in the middle. I don't think it's an oversight, I simply believe that either there was no measurable data or maybe he'd not lived it. Here are the strategies that helped me make the leap to courageous action in my own life.

The Spite Bridge: Spite, for all of its negative connotations and its rightful place in The Dark, helped me through much of The Dark through a personal will to prove the doubters in my life wrong. I wanted to bridge over to The Light, but some people were unsupportive or didn't understand my needs. I was still reliant on them as friends and a support system, and ultimately was tired of them breaking me down. I wanted better, but felt stuck. As a version of fuel, I made my decisions and used their negativity to my advantage by turning it into positive self-speak. This does not fall far from anger or pride, but when fueled with positivity and self-belief, spite can be a powerful ally in bridging to The Light. Be careful, and know that spite has limitations. It is not possible to practice unconditional love while operating in spite. With that said, you can love someone and still leave them in your past if they are unable to support your personal changes. All grievances must be forgiven, so this fuel has an end. In the short term, used wisely, and tied to your why, there may be no faster way to escape the grip of The Dark.

Fake it till you make it: Fake it till you make it is not always a process of positivity. You may feel like there are pieces and parts of the current you that feel like an act. It may still feel like you are lying by trying to be the person you desire to be. If you decide to be positive, or at least act the part, and you are taking the time to be aware of the negative self-speak, you will reprogram your mind towards the positive and the negative will fade away in time. Think of this as feeding your Wolf of Love. This requires choice and an effort to reprogram your mind to realize the truth in who you want to be over the current state of your consciousness. There is both light and dark in this, but it works, and as in all life's struggles positivity prevails. Furthermore, there are multiple studies that point to the fact that it works. As it turns out, we *can* fake it until we make it, and those pieces that feel like an act become part of us over time.

In order to get out of the turmoil of my childhood, I utilized a fake it until you make it attitude. It was predominantly based in spite, but because I was acting in a way that made my brain believe I was getting better, I actually got better. Inside, I sometimes felt like a fraud, but if you imagine a state of being, your natural tendency to want to be correct will drive you directly to that state without pause and through any obstacle. Time also helps; it takes twenty-one days to create a new habit. Imagine that in only twenty-one days you can eliminate your negative self-speak. What would that do for you? You can trick your mind; you can fake it until you make it!

It's important to own our personal recoveries to remain forgiving and patient with others. As you launch into healing, pursuing self-love you may begin to expect others to think as you think. You cannot control others, but please realize that your positivity is affecting those around you at a subconscious level.

EMOTIONAL INTELLIGENCE

There are two primary goals within emotional intelligence for Empaths. The first goal is being aware of the society around you. This is not limited to the constant stream of thoughts, but is deeper than that. This chapter will delve into how you can tap into your awareness of society and how you can control your reaction to it. For definitional purposes, Social Awareness is perceiving what others think and feel through listening and observing, in our case it may go a bit deeper. The key is to be able to practice Social Awareness without taking it personally. Once we are able to enjoy, or at least understand, the society around us, then we are able to build relationships. Relationships are a result of how well you understand a group or individual, and how you are then able to interact with them in a meaningful way. As you may often feel what they feel and know what they know, Empaths have an unrivaled ability to build and maintain relationships. We must be able to conduct these relationships with personal boundaries so that we are not taken advantage of or manipulated due to our trusting nature. This is why it's important that we conduct our relationships with a steady approach. The other person may simply think, "They just get me," but we know better.

Emotional intelligence is where we as Empaths can really struggle. We get stuck in the emotional reaction to our thoughts within the limbic area of the brain and don't practice self-compassion by slowing the process and listening to our needs. Because of this, the second goal is to learn how to avoid getting stuck in our own thought process. We have ample opportunities to practice, and the old adage of practice makes perfect applies just as well to Empaths as it does your day-to-day work. The goal is to build the neuropathways to train your brain. This will then expand its scope and speed. Many people don't realize that your brain is a responsive organ, and it can be trained and manipulated into different strengths through meditation, positivity, focus, and process. The first step is to slow the process moving past the limbic regions, if only for a second, at which point you are already engaging your Neo-Cortex. Then label the feeling, and begin tracking your tendencies towards this feeling, or feelings like it.

Most emotions hinge on happiness, joy, pride, sadness, anger, fear, and shame, and it does not need to be any more complex than that. It is important to not name an emotion as good or bad. Name it for the exact feeling, but stay away from the general terms of good or bad. Instead, focus on the experience as "My experience is…, has made me feel…, and leads me to believe…." The reason for this is imagination presents conflict, if we are to believe something is good or bad allowing room for imagination to grow, we will make the bad come true in our lives, and obsess in the good (Bricks and Balloons). Obsession in the good could be someone working in too much of a good thing, or overcompensating, there is most likely a counterbalance (segment of The Dark) that is being masked. Labeling emotion puts you squarely in Neo Cortex land, as you are processing things as your own, and through practice, you are building the speed and bandwidth of the process.

Once you are efficient at labeling, then we want to explore personal tendencies and identify triggers. What are the hot button issues or feelings that really get to you? For me, it's a sense of loneliness, especially once I've cut someone out of my life that was not healthy. Even though I know it was a toxic relationship, and I was better off without the individual in my life, there seems an emotional hangover that clouds my days. There is relief from this in the finality of your action, and time truly does heal all wounds. In the meantime, control the things you can. You can control you, and your attitudes towards and identification of this trigger is often all that is needed to dismiss it and move forward. Always remember that your personal wellbeing is first, you need to practice compassion towards yourself if you intend to be ready to provide compassion towards others.

If you read the online article base, there is a lot of talk about grounding. These are articles that I'm drawn to, because they are all about the practice of slowing the process and engaging the Neo Cortex. Make grounding personal by seeking out energies that are pleasant to you and disperse the negative energy from you. This is foundational "me time," and the beginnings of meditation. I'm a huge proponent of grounding, as long as the focus remains personally internal. Grounding through exercise is particularly potent, because your body and mind receive dual benefit. Find a cardio you love, as this level of activity relaxes the mind, releases endorphins, dopamine, and serotonin, keeping you happy and alert.

One of my versions of grounding is to finish my thoughts with a positive. By ultimately controlling the positive nature of your self-speak, you can address your emotions and provide new light and context to whatever you originally felt or processed. Think of it as painting over a previous image on canvas with white, and then starting over. This time you're building the same image, but through a different light, and with colors that are pleasing to your eye. Perspective is truly a superpower, and viewing things as a positive, beautifully painted opportunity, or challenge will change the image in your mind. If you are to master this ability, you'll no longer see something as a problem, but rather an opportunity for self-growth and enlightenment.

Being an Empath is like this, it's not a problem, but a beautiful and amazing ability to help and heal the world, one person at a time, through the compassion and understanding that is core to your ability. This gift starts with you, so replace your negative self-speak like "I'm so worthless" with "I feel worthless, but I know I'm not." Trade out "I'm such an idiot" in favor of "I made a mistake, but I also learned from it." Changing the context to something that is not damaging to the self takes the pressure off of you, and it's not a personal attack. It's just another opportunity. Soon, the impulse to speak negatively will lose ground and simply fade away.

To take this a step further, our brains cannot tell the difference between something imagined or real-life input. This provides great personal power if you imagine the best-case scenario and train your brain to focus on that first. It's difficult to do, because we are hard-wired to focus on threats within the limbic area of our brain first. So, flipping this takes time, patience, and effort. We also have a tendency to drive results directly towards our expectations, because we want to be right. If we are focused on a best-case scenario result, then the likelihood of that result coming true is far greater, because you won't expect to let yourself down. This is also why a fake it until you make it perspective works.

Here is a list of strategies that an Empath can use to slow the process down.

1. Journal your thoughts and your reactions to those thoughts.

2. Diagnose how you react to an emotion, understand where it goes within you after your initial reaction, and then pause and try to not react to your reaction.

3. Try to change the context in how you see things. Perspective is a superpower, and a problem is an opportunity.

4. Know that feelings are neither Bad nor Good, they are just feelings, and can leave as quickly as they arrive.

5. Negative reactions generally start to show physical signs in the stomach. As an Empath, your gut instinct is usually right. This is your truth center working on your behalf. Consider muscle testing (discussed below); your body tells you these things in real time, and often it's your stomach that reacts first.

6. Ground in a personally meaningful way while concentrating on your surroundings and breathing rhythm.

7. Walk into discomfort (the fire) and fall back on your personal values.

STRONGER IN YOUR TRUTH

Being an Empath is not a choice, but being a balanced and healthy Empath is. Stay honest, and your truth will follow. Stay humble, and you'll never lose it. Truth is always simple, and right versus wrong is often found in the least common denominator between truth and honesty. When we look for truth, we can find it in the most simplistic of terms, for it requires no explanation. When we are honest, we are being true to ourselves.

I want to draw a line between Honesty and Truth. I see Honesty as an internal battle. With Honesty we can play a game, fold to our internal biases about the world, and convince ourselves that we are being honest even if the outside world may not see us as truthful. Truth is an external concept, and in discussing this I see it in the view of Universal Truth where concepts span different cultures and come to the same truth. Because Truth is more collaborative, when I speak about truth and honesty I don't want you to double down, fold to internal bias, and cheat the process. I want you to take a collaborative look at it with your whole being, Empathic, subconscious, etc., and be truthful, not stubborn. Once you bring bias into the exercise you will engage choice and may cause false results.

Being an Empath, you may commonly feel like you are being hijacked from your own train of thought, or even your moods. It's important to realize that your thoughts may not be your own, so it's equally important to surround yourself wisely. I would like to provide you a very valuable sorting tool that will help you to determine your needs and help to form a personal strategy for being an Empath. I call it 'Fact or Crap?' I love playing Fact or Crap with the thoughts in my head. I think in the long term this is the most valuable piece of advice. I regularly get stuck thinking, "I don't know," and have to reason myself out of it. To get back to me, I'll ask myself, "Was it my question?" If not, then it's filed away as Crap and summarily dismissed. Here is how it works: As you receive messaging, you'll need a filing and sorting system for them.

Track back to your initial thought process, ask yourself, "where am I?" This forces you to collect information about your surroundings, making playing Fact or Crap possible. Surroundings can include physical locations and the details of those location. Fact or Crap uses those details to ground you in the setting and your personal situation. It's a test of personal awareness. You can use almost anything. The size or purpose of the room. The color on the walls. If you are sitting, the fabric or make of the furniture. Is it smooth, coarse, hard, soft? If you are standing, are you standing on tile, wood, carpet? What are its characteristics? Just take stock of the things you have clear understanding of, then address the question in your mind.

Do the same exercise with the thought, trying to ground it in the reality of your setting. This may include: Is this my thought? How did I get to this thought? Am I able to draw a line of reasoning from my prior mental state or thought to this? Do I have any history with this feeling or thought? Can I personally connect to this thought or feeling? Then filter down a bit more. Do I have any personal reason to feel angry, sad, or distraught? At the very moment you have a shred of personal reality and are able to dismiss it as Crap, do so as quick as possible. There is no reason to allow these things to linger around. Then, make efforts to regain your personal composure, focus on what is good in your life and the things you have direct control over.

Once strong enough, you may find great pleasure in scanning the room to try to figure out where it came from. Through the thought and by reading the expressions of others, you can commonly figure it out much like an emotional detective. Sometimes this person may be open. I'm not saying that you should inject yourself into their world or become best friends with them. With that said, complimenting their shoes, shirt, or bag can go a long way. Can you think of a moment when someone else dropped a compliment on you at just the right time? This is something that you can pay forward and, much of the time, bring someone up just a little. If you play this out, this small gesture also brings you up. It lightens their load, which you are open to, thereby lightening your load. Not only is this good for the other individual, but you get the benefit of a dopamine rush that makes you feel good in the process.

Another way to play Fact or Crap is to gauge your personal level of interest in any projected outcome. This works if it's a specific feeling, but does not work well with general feelings. Think about the thought downline or the progression of the thought, and then, as simplistically as possible, play it out. If you have no reason to follow the progression, then it's not yours and you can label it Crap.

Another key factor is, the more general the thought or feeling, the more difficult it is to trace, and the higher the probability that it is not yours. If you cannot explain why you feel a certain way, then it's most likely an Empathic feeling that you are channeling. Channeling is when you are taking on something external and reinforcing it as your own. Constant awareness of your mood, and the ability to understand your personal reason for any mood, is very important. Once you have this personal understanding and are tracking the progression of your feelings, then you will not be so easily swayed by the general mood of society or that family member who is really hard to shake off. Furthermore, you will be able to draw a distinct line between you and them.

Once you are able to diagnose any feeling or thought as originating from a source outside of yourself, take into consideration a cord cutting ritual that is in common use. Just corner the thought in your mind, and think: "I am not them; they are over there; I am over here." This draws a cognitive line between you and the thought. Then, leave it in that corner to dissipate, and move on with your day. It becomes important over time to address each one as they come up, and not try to build personality walls as a barrier.

If drawing the cognitive line doesn't work and you are not in emotional detective mode and curious about where it came from, then you need to make a decision (Fact or Crap). Once you have dismissed it, you allow yourself the freedom to move forward. I personally decide to smile and focus on something that makes me happy, usually my dog. I have an Empathic connection with him that can overpower about anything. This way I'm able to connect with him from anywhere, to wash away the lingering emotions of being Empathic and the original thought. Over time, this also trains the brain to lessen the impact of the intrusion and to focus on love.

If it's Fact, it's yours, and I encourage you to address fact by walking through the fire with additional strategies discussed below.

MUSCLE TESTINGS

Another way to play Fact or Crap is a bit more scientific, and is commonly referred to as Muscle Testing. You may have also heard this referred to as Applied Kinesiology. The basis of the science is that you are physically weaker in a lie. You are therefore stronger in your personal truth, and this can help you asses the validity of your thoughts. Think of a professional athlete on the biggest stage, whether they achieve greatness or sink into a slump often is determined by their mental state. This is why sports psychology is a science as it relates to strength and therefore can be uncovered through muscle testing. Understanding this allows us to connect with our internal strength through honesty. In muscle testing, your body links to your subconscious and will tell you upon inquiry as to the honesty of the statement provided. The body responds in the following way: honesty releases endorphins strengthening the body, and falsehood releases adrenaline, aligning with fear and survival, or your fight or flight response, weakening the body.

Here are a couple of testing methods. The original method of muscle testing devised requires two people, but over time, different, somewhat less accurate, techniques have been developed so that you can work on your own. The original two-person technique requires the subject to elevate their arm out from their side at a 90-degree angle. This isolates their deltoid. The tester applies slight pressure to the top of the outstretched hand, and the subject applies just enough resistance to keep the hand elevated and level. The tester will begin to question the subject using Yes/No or short question statements such as: The sky is blue? (The arm remains strong as the participant states "Yes"). The sky is purple? (The arm dips slightly as the participant states "Yes"). Our bodies inevitably respond with a weakened state when we reply with a false response. This is also the basis for lie detector tests which measure the body's response to questions of the same format. Since we don't always want to invite people into our lives to interrogate us, over time there have been self-testing strategies developed. Please keep in mind these are slightly less accurate.

My personal favorite self-testing method is as follows: interlock your thumb and forefinger in each hand while creating a chain between your two hands. Your thumbs and fingers should be able to pull against each other with some amount of force. Pull as hard as you can maintain while stating an obvious truth such as your name. "My name is [Your Name]." You'll find that you should be able to hold the pressure between your fingers and that it may even become easier. Then, repeat the exercise while stating an obvious lie. "My name is [Pick one that is not yours]." Chances are you weren't able to hold the grip; that is, unless you are really stubborn and choose to cheat the exercise. This is why the self-testing options are a little less accurate. There is a gap when you know in advance that you are going to lie. You still automatically become weaker upon the lie, but the ability to double down and grip tighter has a bit more choice involved than when a tester is questioning you. This is that line we've discussed between honesty and truth (internal bias), so when testing, it's important to perform the exercise truthfully.

You may also find this strategy helpful in discovering who you really are. Start with something easy like music. Listen to your playlists, and use muscle testing to determine your favorite songs, or those that may cause you pain. This is a private and realistic way to practice, and it may also reveal unrealized preferences or traits about you. One of those favorite songs may have lost its luster or may have a negative association to someone. Once you are comfortable with addressing things in your life, start to assess your fears. You may have taken on a fear of the storm as taught within your childhood, but actually like the sound of thunder and rain as you sleep. Once you have practiced on the impersonal items on your life, catalogue your relationships. Your true friends will inevitably rise to the top, and your strength will make that clear.

It's a very helpful self-knowledge tool that can assist you in your journey. With practice you can feel the chemical change produced by a lie and stay honest. The phrase "a pit in my stomach" originates here; we are evolutionarily programmed to feel deceit, fear, and great emotion in our stomachs. This is the body's way of telling you to run, ralph, or fight.

Honesty is a personal fight; only you can control you. That's not to say you should work at it without a support system or friends by your side. You may begin to filter these individuals out using muscle testing as an aid. Take the time to categorize the people in your life, know who your allies are and who those people who provide negative influence are. You know your true friends and family; these are your support system. It may also be a mentor, meeting, support group, or religious institution. There is no wrong answer, but going it alone does increase the hardships of walking through the fire. This refers to the practice of humility. Your decisions are yours, but you can source the strength to love yourself, through the love provided to you by others. Seeing in yourself what others see in you can take time, introspection, and patience. This perspective, patience, and positivity is the very thing that you need to move into your new house of positivity.

Positivity is important, as the body goes weak in a state of doubt, unhealthy emotional attitude, or mental stress. As an Empath, the state of society and your ability to sense it can have profound impact on your mental wellbeing. Additionally, stress is ultimately generated by the attitudes toward the circumstance the feeling is generated from. This means that being upset that you are an Empath is not a viable solution. The alternative is turning being an Empath into a strength. If someone looks at a situation as a hindrance, the body will inevitably become weak. If someone were to look at a situation as a challenge, that will inevitably make them stronger. Being an Empath is a challenge, there is no doubt about that. Viewing it as such is a pivotal moment of healing.

FORGIVENESS

As an Empath, it's important to forgive the intrusion of others. They know not what they do, they are just living in their personal space, putting a frequency into the world without knowledge that there is a receiver for that frequency. That receiver, like it or not, is you, and those frequency broadcasts are a part of you. It will be incredibly difficult to make improvements to your own life if you are constantly inconvenienced by receiving those frequencies. If you are frustrated by something that is part of you and there is no means of cutting it out, then you must come to terms with it. This includes, but is not limited to, forgiving the intrusion of others in your mental stream of consciousness. This is a first and necessary step to personal serenity.

To forgive others, and more importantly to forgive yourself, without further ridicule or judgement is to be given the gift of freedom. Those imaginary bindings that you put on others or on past circumstance don't actually punish others. Those bindings can only hurt you, as you are the deciding factor as to their existence and placement. They hold you in the past, unable or unwilling to move forward into a beautiful potential life. Many people don't realize that they are indeed the deciding factor as to their own happiness, and much of the time forgiveness is the key. Forgive them for you, and/or forgive yourself for them. If forgiveness is completed in a truthful way, freedom from past pain is immediate and lasting. Please know that self-compassion and selfishness through forgiveness are not the same thing. Compassion for the self is how we prepare ourselves to give compassion to others. You can't give something away that you don't already have.

In cases of lost life where you are trying to hold on, in all of my spiritual experience I've not run into a single situation where the lost want you to hold on. They know the damage of this, and want you to live to your greatest potential, as they are on the side of love. Forgive you for you! Once completed, this provides you the freedom of self-love and releases the negativity in your life that ultimately only damages your sense of self.

As an Empath you are half-way there, but you must be self-compassionate. You are your greatest friend, and forgiveness of the self is the way forward to joy. Joy is the way forward to true healing. Please realize that the past is the past, and your now is your future. There may be challenges that remain from past decisions, but walk through the fire with honesty as your guide and find your peace.

HO'OPONOPONO

Ho'oponopono is a mediation tradition originating in the Hawaiian culture. It is said to be an essential piece of Huna, a spiritual and healing custom, originally performed by shamans honoring the spirits. It was also used as an interpersonal mediation technique between tribal members in a dispute to restore harmony and balance. It is a very simple tool that over time has been personalized to rid an individual of harmful memories that hold us back in life from our true potential. It is a practice that re-establishes personal, mental, and physical balance and promotes Qi. The purpose is to free our tormented selves from our past memories, limiting beliefs, and future reactions that will damage our wellbeing. For definition, a harmful memory can be a slight, personal or external, that we create based on judgement. These are circumstances that we have held on to and imprisoned within our Personality Walls. In this way it's a valuable tool for reprograming our subconscious.

Our goal is to heal the parts of ourselves that create harmful situations in our lives, thereby limiting our reactions that damage us little by little, in place of the ongoing and ever deepening cycles of frustration stemming from the original slight that cause the current subliminal sabotage. With Ho'oponopono, we can address and wash our past of these hauntings. The great thing about Ho'oponopono is it only requires you, is performed on your schedule, and is up to you to correct the immediate need or circumstance (harmful memory) that you reacted to.

It is truly easy as an Empath to play the victim; it's almost required that you feel that this bombardment is not your fault. We naturally look outwards for a stimulus to place blame upon, and at the same time imprison ourselves. This is hard-wired into us as part of our fight or flight mechanism. As this is a natural reaction, it's difficult to not judge others and/or yourself within the process. Proceeding in a way controlled by our hard wiring leads us to simply try to survive, because we have given our responsibility away, and within that, our personal power over the situation. This leaves us exposed, and we begin to judge ourselves because we feel powerless. It's important to realize that we are in control of our own outcome. It's important to realize that asking for and receiving forgiveness is not because we are guilty of something past or present. It's important to understand that at the end of our lives we are responsible for 100% of that life and its outcome. As we shrink this down into a moment, and every moment thereafter, we are 100% responsible for each moment, each thought, and therefore each outcome. Much of this has to do with our reactions to those situations. To truly balance and heal we are required to take 100% responsibility for what we think, feel, and react, as your perception of all things creates your world.

We all have a past, and these are long roads laid over time that have made us who we are. These experiences are most likely labeled as good or bad experiences, but this labeling requires a level of judgement and this is a mistake. This judgement is the power behind a harmful memory, and it controls you and your reactions at a subconscious level to all other experiences in your life. This creates conflict, because your present is then controlled by the subconscious slights of your past, and these thoughts continue and push to grow until they become limiting factors in your life, creating a vicious cycle of fear. We often don't even remember the instigating circumstance because it could have been so small, but the growth of it over time has overshadowed the reality of the situation. We also believe what we think because we want to be right. If we think, "I'm worthless," our reality and perspective of the world will seek out situations to reinforce the thought.

This is where Ho'oponopono comes in. It allows you in real time, in the moment of reaction, to defuse the harmful memory. It's simple, direct, silent, and private. It takes but a couple of seconds and you are in complete control, because as we discussed you are 100% responsible for each moment of your life, past, present, and future.

The practice of Ho'oponopono is to ask your spirit, your subconscious self, for forgiveness for the intrusion of this memory. I've found this to be wonderful for clearing out my Empathic space as well, because in Empathic situations I'm able to own my reaction and cleanse my personal space. The premise, and phrase is simple. "I'm sorry, forgive me, thank you, I love you." This is the phrase that we internally recite upon the intrusion of a harmful memory, filling in details if we deem necessary. If this memory happens to be an Empathic intrusion, so be it, it's still yours, you still own it. As we forward this line of thinking to our relationships as Empaths, and because we lead with our hearts, we are predisposed to give away our power. In our case this is love; we want to take care of others, but at the cost of personal sacrifice. By owning the Empathic thought, you retain power over it, and can control the outcome while maintaining the energy needed to take care of yourself, and, if you choose, the other individual as well.

Let's break it down: practice makes (perfect) purification.

"I'm sorry" – This means that you are taking responsibility for the intrusion. You are internalizing compassion for yourself because you are personally sorry for the intrusion. "I'm sorry that this harmful memory has grazed this moment." This is to take the place of your programed reaction to the harmful memory. Where our programed self may respond with "I'm such an idiot," we are now going to stop that reaction with "I'm sorry." It's clean, honest, patient, and compassionate. It's a wonderful gift in a moment of anguish.

114

"Forgive me" – This request for forgiveness is from the now, for the harmful memory has risen up from our subconscious selves and because we did not manage it in the moment it existed, it's come back to haunt us in this moment. I'm a big fan of second chances, and this is that moment. By forgiving ourselves for the existence of the harmful memory we free ourselves from any remaining guilt that we may have towards it. By asking for forgiveness, you are cleansing the harmful memory and clearing your path.

"Thank you" – This is an acknowledgement of your second chance, and an acknowledgement that you deserve the second chance. You are so thankful to have the opportunity to heal yourself and cleanse this harmful memory from your subconscious that you must provide yourself thanks. This thankfulness acknowledges that you have moved past the harmful memory, washing it from your subconscious, leaving it to dissipate from the now.

"I Love you" – We all deserve love, but self-love is the most important kind. How we see ourselves in each moment of our lives is defined by this love. You just successfully neutralized and dissipated a harmful memory from your personal past. This act of personal power of reclamation deserves both thanks and love. You can now stand a little bit taller, and walk forward into your future moments knowing that this harmful memory has been washed away. You have reclaimed that piece of you, and love yourself for it.

All of this in a short phrase that does all of the work for you. Using it in your Empathic space does just the same. Imagine an Empathic intrusion, and walk through the phrasing again. "I'm sorry, forgive me, thank you, I love you." It allows you the moment to breathe, collect yourself, and not take it personally. Furthermore, it absolves you of reaction, and within the same moment allows you to take responsibility of letting go of the intrusion forever. It's a highly effective and beautiful gift to yourself. If there are multiple harmful memories within a single circumstance, then address each individually.

I like to use a shorter version of this to acknowledge self-praise. If I happen to compliment myself (outside of the scope of ego), I'll think; "Thank you, I love you." I preface outside of the scope of ego, for ego is not complimentary, but destructive self-speak that holds you back by elevating yourself through judgement of others. I've also created a trick that plays well with the outside world. When I say; "Thank you," I think "I love you." It doesn't matter the recipient. Sometimes it's the checkout guy at the grocery store, other times it's the stranger on the street that held a door for my benefit. There's something about it that changes the reaction of the individual. All of this taking place at a subconscious vibrational level, it seems to elevate the words "Thank you" to the level of "I love you" without cause for alarm. The result is a calm peace provided to a stranger and their response is reciprocal without knowledge. I've also found this to be helpful when there is tension within my familial relationships; a simple "Thank you" with intent of "I love you" diffuses a moment without knowledge. Try this out next time a family member is pushing your buttons. The thought matters far more than the words. The way we read vibrations in our family relations also matters more than the words.

EFT – EMOTIONAL FREEDOM TECHNIQUE

EFT – Emotional Freedom Technique is a manipulation of certain meridian points that free Qi, releasing blockages and freeing you from emotional triggers. I love it because it takes the positives of acupuncture and meridians and combines it with the benefits of practices such as Ho'oponopono. EFT has long been used to treat Post Traumatic Stress Disorder (PTSD) and has been shown to release anxiety through manipulation of meridian points. I like to practice this along with Ho'oponopono; it's a nice build-upon practice, as in EFT we corner thoughts and utilize mental forgiveness. We also build our own self speak. I recommend a base of Ho'oponopono, as getting used to that phrasing can be useful at times where full EFT cycles may be inconvenient. Although neither Ho'oponopono nor EFT were built to go together, I've found that combining the practices yields great results.

Here are the steps:

1. Corner the thought.

2. Test the intensity of the thought. Assign it a number on a scale of 1-10, 10 being most disturbing. Do not label it as good or bad, rather name it what it is.

3. Phrase it within positive self-speak. While building your mantra (summary of the trauma utilizing positive self-speak), repeat this phrasing as you tap the small intestine meridian at the SI 3 meridian point. I like to build the details of the trauma into Ho'oponopono as the base phrasing "I'm sorry, forgive me, thank you, I love you." This ensures your phrasing remains positive and provides grounding.

4. Tap through these points while repeating your chosen phrasing.

5. Small intestine meridian SI 3 - If you were to karate chop something, this is the connection point. Along your pinkie between the pinkie and wrist joint. It's known to open up the spine and relieve pain in your joints. Tap this within the building of you mantra (number three) as listed above.

6. Governing vessel GV 20 – The top and center of your head where your two skull plates meet. Manipulates mental concentration and memory.

7. Urinary bladder meridian UB 2 – The inside point of your eyebrow. Known to assist in balanced breathing.

8. Gallbladder meridian GB 1 – This is the spot otherwise known as your temple, just behind the outside of your eyebrow in the basin of the bone. Known to assist in digestion and headaches.

9. Stomach meridian ST 1 – This is a spot located just under your eye. Known to assist in vision.

10. Governing vessel GV 26 – Located just under your nose, above your top lip. Used to treat mental conflict and restore calm.

11. Conception vessel CV 24 – Just under the lower lip in the depression above your chin. A meeting point for stomach, large intestine, and governing channels. Known to assist in mouth related and radiating pain.

12. Kidney meridian KD 27 – Just below your collarbone in the space between your sternum and top rib. Known to assist in level breathing, chest pain, and vomiting.

13. Spleen meridian SP 21 – For the ladies, it's located where the bottom of your bra touches below your arm pit. For the guys, about four fingers below your nipple where your pinkie would be under your arm pit. Known to assist in breathing, aching and weakness of the limbs.

14. Test the intensity of the thought again. Assign it a number on a scale of 1-10, 10 being most disturbing. Repeat as necessary to bring the disturbance number to neutral.

I want to take this opportunity to introduce a couple of self-care points that, in addition to those mentioned above, can be helpful in alleviating emotional stress. When used together and incorporated into self-care, these points can help in overcoming physical and mental pain. There is no need for acupuncture needles; simply squeezing or tapping on these points can release energies to optimum flow, calming the body.

1. Heart meridian HT 7 – Located on the wrist crease on the pinkie side of the hand. Used to instill calm to the heart, treat fright, and irritability.

2. Large Intestine meridian LI 4 – Located in the gap between your thumb and pointer finger. This is a headache and pain treatment point. Pressing here assists with pain in the head and face, and instills calm. I often use LI 4 when in stressful meetings.

3. Spleen meridian SP 6 – Located inside of your leg, four finger widths up your leg from the top bone in your ankle. My favorite point because it's a crossing point for the Spleen, Kidney, and Liver meridians. Used to treat many things including insomnia, headache, and dizziness.

4. Liver meridian Li 3 – Located between your big toe and second toe at the upper-most point. I've heard this referred to as the

happiest point in the body. Used to release negative energies and treat liver disorders, including damage by alcohol.

5. Pericardium meridian PC 6 – Located two inches above the inside of the wrist joint between the tendons. Used to treat nausea.

6. Triple Energizer TE 5 – Located on the opposite side of the wrist from PC 6 – Responsible for releasing stagnant Qi between the upper and lower bodies. Used to treat digestion and pain. I use this and PC 6 in tandem, squeezing both sides of the wrist.

7. Gall Bladder meridian GB 41 – Located on the outside, top middle of your foot. Used to treat eye spasms and migraine pain.

8. Yin Tang is located at the midpoint between the eyebrows. Used to relieve headaches and various discomforts of the face. This point is widely acclaimed to help your cares simply fade away.

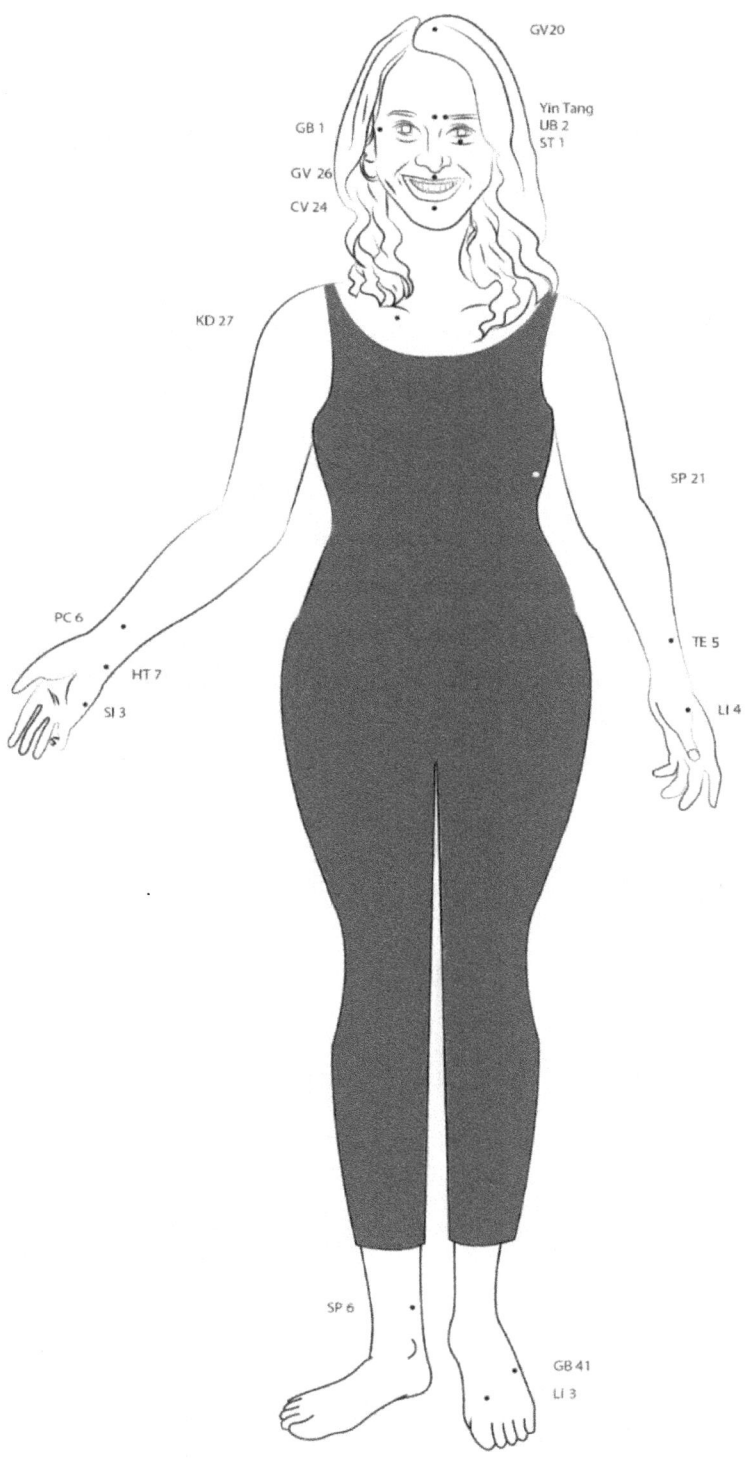

GV20

Yin Tang
UB 2
ST 1

GB 1

GV 26

CV 24

KD 27

SP 21

PC 6

TE 5

HT 7

SI 3

LI 4

SP 6

GB 41

LI 3

An additional manual manipulation trick to use in a moment of stress is to engage your thalamus. The thalamus may be manipulated through pressure by tapping just above your breastbone. Doing this while delivering positive thoughts can have profound impact on real time mood and energy. This can be used to assist you with muscle testing to provide additional clarity and strength. You can also use this technique real time in moments of stress, to reprogram a response and regulate your physical chemical makeup.

Prior to writing this book, I had limited knowledge and no ability to provide acupuncture as selfcare. Since delving into this world, I've found it magical that a point in the top of your foot can make you feel relaxed and happy, or that a point between my eyebrows can help to clear my mind. As I continued to provide self-care my family took notice, and now I provide basic care to my little ones, treating headaches, night terrors, and sports recovery. I know as a family our reliance on pain medication, and even cold medication, has reduced.

THE ENERGY OF A LIFE

The source of our reality is our frame of experience, creating our scope of understanding. Seeing as humans live as a collective society, if one person makes a personal improvement, then this brings up the entire collective. As Empaths, we have the ability to sense others, to imagine the sick becoming healthy, the hateful becoming loving, and how that would create a sense of peace worldwide. This would obviously benefit you, but it would also be to the benefit of all living.

How we resonate with the world around us can be in harmony, or it can be toxic. We can also pick up the resonance of others, as life is not a closed loop. Bones, cartilage, tendons, ligaments, and fascia are all crystalline in structure, and are meant to conduct the energies of life. They can also receive and conduct the energies of the world around you. What I've noticed through my personal growth is, the weaker your personal signal, the greater your susceptibility to the signals of others. Everything and everyone gives off an energy pattern that resonates as a frequency specific to that thing, plant, animal, or individual. This energy pattern can be received by everyone, but is read and absorbed primarily by those who know how or are gifted. As an Empath, you intuitively know how; fine tuning this into a skill that can be controlled, or at least understood, will be a positive in your life.

Empathy is the foundation of any meaningful relationship - to feel something that someone else is going through and provide compassion is a bonding agent that spans all cultures and species of the world. Empathy is also karmic, in that if you provide compassion and kindness, these will then return back to you. This cyclical relationship building is a spiritual practice, it's the ability to feel the presence of someone else through their emotions, pain, or joy. As they may feel your presence, they may set reasonable boundaries for their experience. As an Empath, do your best to respect these boundaries, as it's ok to know and not say. Find a time when approachability allows support, and pick those times wisely.

The consciousness of all living things is a transmitter and receiver for energy patterns - most immediately those of your own body in the form of thought. Babies and children know their connection to their mother and father far prior to birth; it's biological, and this is the source of our Empathic abilities. Children don't lose or reduce this ability until later in life when communication patterns change to fit mainstream society. We are, however, born into an Empathic communication mode, and our brains are wired to be part of the collective that is our parental bond. Our brains don't forget. Many people shut this off unconsciously, while others try shut it off consciously, which is far more difficult because we are then choosing imbalance and attempting to block others out. This will inevitably result in sickness, be it mental or physical. The mind is meant to communicate, and will remain a receiver regardless of conscious fight or flight.

Think of this as if everyone has their own radio station. All of the lower frequencies are free, and provide no upfront cost or work to obtain. Above that are paid subscription levels that do require work to obtain. The karmic portion of this is that the signal band you transmit is also the signal band that you are most likely to receive. If you are operating one of the lower bands, then you are by default receiving all of the radio advertisements from everyone else at that level too. The only way to graduate from all of the spam is to pay (walk through the fire) the subscription cost for the higher frequency.

You are more likely to receive signals from others that are operating at the same level as you. This means that if you are distraught with guilt, you will also be taking on the guilt of others. When you rise above these levels you will be shedding a positive balancing light on those who are operating at lower levels, and will also be taking on the strength of your peers at the higher levels. It's a self-benefiting system, and you are also balancing and leading those who are in The Dark.

Animal empathy – All animals are Empaths; their primary mode of communication is through this channel. As they say, "Animals smell fear." They also sense love, compassion, illness, and loss. Anyone who has ever had a pet stay at their side when home for a sick day knows this truth. This aligns with my experience, and given some ability, all animals can be connected with, although each has a slightly different frequency. Animals cannot lie or exaggerate the truth. They are honest in all emotions because they are innocent enough to live in the moment at most times. They don't allow their imaginations to control their long term well-being, although they do suffer in times of change and loss like anyone else. This is why we gravitate towards having pets and keeping them as family. They feel what we feel, and naturally embrace family in our times of need.

Donors – I have living bone from other souls in my body, and daily rely on their strength and charity. I don't know if I can feel them on a regular basis because they are so ingrained with me. I like to think that I was given the benefit of a stronger, more diverse energy signature. I've also read stories about how recipients of heart transplants take on personality traits, memories, and even food preferences of the donor. The recipients report familial ties with the donor's family as if they were their own, even if they had never met prior to the transplant. What I do know is that when people check the donor box, their act of charity is an act of unconditional love.

Past souls - Many Empaths obtain this skill accidentally. My ability to commune with past souls has gotten stronger and far clearer through my life. This ends up being a related subject, because if we are able to pick up the vibration of the living, that vibration can continue to communicate with you after death. As we are continuously causing vibration in our life through continuous movement those energies continue on forever. Just like a hurricane that began as the flap of a butterfly wing, or the ripple effect of a stone being cast into still waters, our energies continue on. I also like to think that our soul continues to cast energy and, through this, communicate with the living world. The Chinese culture writes of this, considering death as a graduation to being a ruler of the world.

Communing with past souls is slightly different, as many people can be very strong Empaths and completely shut this side of it off. Our consciousness is energy - our signature that survives our body. When this consciousness is aligned with positivity it remains as such, and continues its energy throughout time. The mind transcends the body just as the fear of death is transcended. The release of fear allows freedom in life after death, and within our time on earth. If aligned with a negative outlook, it will remain in this weakened state after death. I've been visited to have conversations, and as such I believe that past souls gravitate to those that can still read their energy. My Empathic nature does not let me forget the energy of a past soul. This is a gift.

If it is within you to have a conversation, have the conversation, and attempt to resolve past conflict. This is a way of walking through the fire, and often the conflict that requires resolution is the very thing that is holding the past soul in place. If you are looking for temporary relief, then grounding, smudging, and sage oil may provide temporary relief. Ultimately, if something requires voice it will need to be said. If a soul has unfinished business it may not be able to let go without resolution. I've found that past souls choose you, not the other way around. If you are consciously closed off, they find you in a dream state since you are more malleable in this moment.

When communing with past souls some people report smells. This makes perfect sense, as smell is so strongly tied to memory that memory can trigger smell and vice versa. Smell is the only one of our senses that bypasses the filing systems of our thalamus, going right to your conscious-driven cerebral cortex. This is why smell and memory are so closely tied.

Please know it's not wise to try to hold onto past souls due to inevitable pain and torment to you both. In the case they need you and you are open, they may check in from time to time, provide peace, and take away negative energy in times of need, freeing you to continue on with strength. With a built relationship, they are then referred to by many cultures around the world as Spirit Guides. This is a sign of Universal Truth.

PERSONAL CARE/THE LIGHT

CHAKRAS, THE LIGHT

"Darkness cannot drive out darkness: only light can do that. Hate cannot drive out hate: only love can do that."

Martin Luther King Jr.

The Chakras, as found in the Indian culture, are an eloquent and beautiful way to describe the path to enlightenment. I want to use them to speak about The Light because they resonate well with the belief system of most Empaths. Although this book is being written primarily from a Chinese perspective, I wanted to confirm a few similarities between the Indian Chakra system and Chinese Medicine theory. First, they both believe in the movement of energy through the meridian system. The Chakras each sit in a pooling site for Prana that, if spinning (like a wheel), will release energy on demand to be used in relation to the Chakra. The Indian concept of Prana is nearly interchangeable with the Chinese Qi. Also similar is the belief in a Yin/Yang system, Yin being to Kudalini (Feminine), and Yang being to Shiva (Masculine). Once again, we see different cultures practicing nearly identical theories with differing terms, pointing to Universal Truth.

Additionally, Western and Eastern societal models speak about a nearly identical progression of enlightenment, leading to another sign of Universal Truth. For comparison: Western society, as based on the writings of David R Hawkins, is scientifically founded, with the use of Kinesiology (Muscle Testing) setting the progression as: Courage, Neutrality, Willingness, Acceptance, Reason, Love, Joy, Peace, and finally Enlightenment. Like David R Hawkins and the research he conducted, Eastern society has a long-standing scale documenting the nature of positivity which details the levels in a slightly different way. This is the Chakra system.

There are many levels of personal energy below that of the Root Chakra, and these are considered unhealthy and a sign of blocked Chakra channels.

We have discussed them as The Dark. These lead to illnesses affecting the mental and physical welfare of the individual, as the negative energies produced damage the body's natural systems. They are low in bioelectric power and make up the vast majority of the human race.

Chakra is a Sanskrit word meaning circle or wheel. Wheel refers directly to the body's energy cycles, mental acuity, the organs, and nerve systems (similar to how meridians and organ networks are described in Chinese Medicine). There are Seven Chakras, they align along the spinal column, and have organ networks and color/vibration significance. If a person has all of their colors in harmony, they will produce white light. If one color falls out of balance within the color wheel, they will no longer be able to maintain white light. If we were to split white light through a prism, we would see the entire color wheel represented in the output. Conversely, it requires a combination of all the colors of the spectrum to produce truly white light. This pure white light is indicative of Enlightenment (Crown). Your energy is no different. It functions on the dispersion of Prana (Positive Energy, Spirit). Prana is another version of Qi, but the two terms result in an understanding of life force, and the proper workings of the body unobstructed.

There is a physical side to each Chakra that ties into the meridian channels as discussed in the Chinese Medicine meridians section. The Chakras in Indian culture are known as the sites along the meridian channels that pool Prana. This aligns nearly identically to the Chinese theory of Qi and the flow of energy. When the Chakra wheels are spinning without obstruction, the body can keep moving forward in good ability and open the door to positive spirit. I believe that this requires the work necessary (diet and exercise) to keep the body in good health.

Then there is the mental side of the Chakra system. Internal work is necessary to keep the benefits of these Chakras. Although the physical wheels may be spinning, the gains from these wheels may not open up in your mind without the work necessary (compassion and forgiveness). When all are open and spinning, the benefits are universal to self and the world.

I make this distinction, as I believe the limitation of the Chakra system is that it is founded on a general state of positivity, beginning with your ability to root into nature and connect with all living things. This idea is foreign to many and, within the scope of our city civilization, is being lost. This means that much of our population is unaware, operating as if independent, and functioning in society with imbalanced meridians and Chakras. Many individuals are living a half-life stemming from doubts and fears, causing blockage that holds them back from a beautiful life. This describes the bulk of society, and the relative state of the world culture discussed as The Dark.

This does not need to be you. In fact, I'm betting that Empaths are the key to a better, more balanced, and more loving world. To affect the few is to affect the many. The mental side of the Chakra system works as a staircase, building to the Crown Chakra (Enlightenment) from The Dark. Upon a sense of personal courage and a willingness to take responsibility for, and to make changes to, their own life, Empaths begin to align with the mental principles of balance within the Chakras. Upon realization of a full series of spinning/open Chakras, there are personal gains in all areas of life including mental stability. This stability fosters a sense of connection with themselves, their surroundings and benefits their relationships.

Muladhara - Root Chakra – Root is, as the name would imply, your base, and is responsible for providing stability as a root system to the world. Root will influence basic needs such as digestion and reproductive health, keeping you full of both energy and a drive for future results. When it is in alignment with your personal sense of truth you will feel rooted, sturdy, and the winds of change will not rock you. You'll operate with a sense of connectedness. Be willing to try new things, and be courageous in the effort. Root also assumes the practice of grounding.

1. Root is your base and sits at the base of your spine.

2. The color association is Red, associated stones include Garnet, Bloodstone, and Ruby. Other color associations align with earth tones as would align with the ability to root (Brown, Black, Grey).

3. Oils for use – Ginger and Cypress. Herbal – Ginseng.

4. Every one person with positive Bio-Energy power aligned with their Root Chakra is able to counterbalance the negative energy of 12 individuals in The Dark.

5. On the David R Hawkins scale, Root aligns with Courage: The level of empowerment and opportunity, as challenges are met with a willingness to try new things. You maintain a positive self-image and open mind. You also maintain an ability to take responsibility for your individual truth.

Svadhishthana - Sacral Chakra – Sacral is your personal wellness, happiness, and creativity Chakra. It also has responsibilities along the lines of desire and pleasure, fueling attractiveness and sexuality. Sacral relies on balance within your personal identity to influence these factors and allow a feeling of connection, allowing intimacy and compassion towards others. When open, you will no longer see things in strict black and white, but will be able find reason in all things. You'll be productive in society and feel security in your personal and romantic relationships, which will thrive. As you are managing your relationships well, this Chakra will birth great creativity.

1. Sacral is associated with the liver, kidneys, spleen, and immune system.

2. Color association is orange, and stones include Citrine and Amber. Copper is considered an amplifier.

3. Oils for use – Sandalwood and Rosewood. Herbal – Calendula.

4. On the David R Hawkins scale, Sacral aligns with Neutrality: A position that does not see things in black and white, and which values freedom. It also aligns with Willingness. Individuals are friendly, outgoing, social, contributors to society.

Manipura – Solar Plexus Chakra – Solar Plexus is your confidence center, and is responsible for intelligence, confidence, and ability to harness your energy towards desired production, as well as courage to move forward. Considered the intelligence Chakra, original meanings were of brilliance and house, referring to the balance of thought dispersing Prana. There is an ingrained personal knowledge that reason and education equal personal capital. When open, you are in a healthy, confident, and energetic state. Respectful to ourselves, there is an internal strength that is rising up, and you are working on discerning truth from all things.

1. Located near the upper abdominal region, associated organs include liver and stomach.

2. Color association is Yellow, and stones include Citrine, Amber, and Tiger Eye.

3. Oils for use – Lemon and Juniper. Herbal – Milk Thistle.

4. On the David R Hawkins scale, Solar Plexus aligns with Reason – Intelligence and rationalism over emotion. Education and knowledge are seen as personal strength.

Anahata – Heart Chakra – Heart represents unconditional love connecting all things and the spirit as one. As an Empath, you naturally reside here, but may be weighed down with many of the prior discussed thoughts and feelings. Once open, you have found that love is self-created. Now free of the bindings of material possession (want or greed), you realize that love may be given and received freely. Furthermore, your love of yourself cannot be taken away by anyone or anything. You've reached this realization through the search for personal truth and your connection to the greater community of life. You forgive yourself and others with ease, and realize that past mistakes do not define the spirit of a person. The Heart Chakra is the healing center, and allows trust in your connection with unconditional love and compassion towards yourself and others. An unconditional and permanent love for others becomes a state of being, and there is no longer a place for hate or greed. This is the beginnings of true compassion towards others without judgement or fear.

1. The Heart Chakra is directly associated with the organ heart.

2. Color association is Green, and stones include Peridot, Jade, Emerald, and Rose Quartz.

3. Oils for use - Pine, Rose, and Jasmine. Herbal – Rose Hips.

4. For every one person who is in the positive Bio-Energy power, with a fully open Heart Chakra, they are able to counterbalance the negative energy of 750,000 individuals who are in The Dark.

5. On the David R Hawkins scale, Heart aligns with Love that is unconditional, unchanging, and permanent. Loving becomes a state of being. You know the fallible nature of the human state, and provide love and forgiveness leading to compassion and grace. Material possessions and personal needs become irrelevant. There is no blame, no hate, and no guilt.

The following are Higher Spiritual Chakras associated with the benefit of all life.

Vishuddha – Throat Chakra – Throat represents purification, and hinges on truth, clarity of mind aligning with truth and honesty, and being able to communicate clearly. There are two segments to honesty and the enlightenment therein. The first is the ability to take responsibility for all things in your life. The second is honesty in communication. When open, there is a creative bridge between you and another's point of view. Both are important to the enlightened state of an Empath, as honesty is the permanent bridge between The Dark and The Light. Once open, material possessions may lose relevance, and there will be a greater focus on helping others through individual financial means. It is realized that personal achievement is bound to contextual perspective, and this perspective is the gateway to health. Moreover, this perspective determines an individual's relative strength over their personal health and power. The realizations are able to be communicated and clarified in the simplest of terms.

1. Throat Chakra is associated with the throat, mouth, and thyroid.

2. Color association is Blue, and stones include Sapphire, Topaz, Turquoise, Aquamarine, and Agate.

3. Oils for use – Lavender, Chamomile, and Geranium. Herbal - Chamomile.

4. On the David R Hawkins scale, Throat aligns with Acceptance: Love is found to be self-created, and it's realized that it cannot be taken away by another. This also entails courage to face your personal truth and to make individual contributions to its positive amplification. There is a significant focus on inclusion with the realization that there is no Us vs Them. There are no tribes or races. There is just Us, and that spans all life, all species.

Ajna – The Third Eye – Representing spiritual awareness, knowledge, and wisdom center. Near death experiences commonly open The Third Eye. When open, the individual has full access to their intuition and self-knowledge in the form of wisdom, knowing, and spiritual joy. They are able to communicate this joy in the simplest of terms, and words fail to hold the gravity of the descriptions. They are able to visualize a better world, and to take steps to make that world a reality. When in alignment, a full host of communicative Empathic abilities come to the surface, but they have the personal strength to fully control, and understand them. Love becomes even more centralized to the individual. This individual lives in a positive state and disperses that positivity to others. Keeping The Third Eye open requires positivity and a focus on the influence of that positivity on the self and others through illumination. This positivity for others can be realized simply through positive thought transference.

1. The Third Eye is associated with the consciousness.

2. Color association is Indigo, and stones include Sodalite, Fluorite, and Quartz.

3. Oils for use - Frankincense and Cedar. Herbal – Skullcap.

4. For every one person who is in the positive bio-energy power, with a fully open Third Eye Chakra, they are able to counterbalance the negative energy of 10,000,000 individuals who are in The Dark.

5. On the David R Hawkins scale, The Third Eye aligns with Joy – Love becomes even more central. Near death experiences can transform people to this state. The Third Eye causes energy to disperse, and this awareness will allow great leaps in consciousness.

Sahasrara – The Crown – Representing a complete open mind, enlightenment, and a one-ness with all. The Crown resides atop the head as an aura or halo would. When open, there is the feeling of divine peace and joy in every moment of life. There is unbounded hope for the world and selflessness in productivity to make the world a peaceful and joyous place. The spreading of this individual's positivity and hope can be centralized to a single individual, but is most regularly mass distributed to the whole population of life. Everything is seen as infinite and connected. Often, the traditional religions of the world are transcended, as they have been muddled through misinterpretation of the foundational message. The original message has been self-realized, and is understood with piercing clarity and enlightenment. There is no longer anything hidden in the world; truth has been received and is evident in all life. This individual will then elevate further, taking unbounded steps to document and move the message along in an effort to positively affect the whole of life.

1. Color associations are white or violet, and stones include White Topaz, Calcite, and Amethyst.

2. Oils for use – Myrrh, Frankincense, and Lavender. Herbal – Valerian.

3. On the David R Hawkins scale, this aligns with Peace: Everything is seen as connected and infinite. Religion is often transcended and replaced with pure spirituality.

To delve a bit deeper into the Indian culture, it also incorporates concepts of differing layers of body.

1. The Physical Body is the tangible body.

2. Etheric Body is your energy field produced by your physical body; this is predominantly physical energy drifting from activity or simply being alive.

3. Astral Body is an emotional connection to your experience. This is

where our emotional energy drifts. When you can see anger, fear, or peace and joy in a person, you are seeing their Astral Body. Empaths can readily feel this layer. We are incredibly in tune with this body as it's also considered aura. This energy can be seen by some, and it's the Chakra color wheel that we emit within this layer.

4. Mental Body (Blue Pearl) is your ideal and belief system, where personal truths are housed. It's our consciousness and, I like to think, where our base intuition lies. It's just outside of our emotional reaction center, and we simply need to pause to access it. It shows itself in light meditation and through choice.

5. The Spiritual Body is the soul of the body. This ties us to our past lives and universal consciousness. This is your Empathic layer that shows itself in dream and deep meditation, and it's what caries us through the afterlife and into future Etheric bodies.

Although I provide stones, oils, and herbals for use within the descriptions above, I want to reinforce that the work to be done is inside of yourself. If you feel that you need assistance in capturing the resonance of any given level, then please utilize these.

I also want to share a personal story. I have a little one that, through ages 2-7, suffered from awful night terrors, and it was to the point that you dare not wake her if she were still sleeping because she was impossibly scared and angry. Within my reading and research, I came across a solution of an Amethyst and Bloodstone combination that was to assist with night terrors. I gave these stones to her, and she tucked them into her pillowcase, I also performed acupuncture on her with specific points to clear related channels.

We've not heard her scream out at night for years, and she says she gets better rest and is more alert. She's pure in that she can feel a difference when they are coming back around. About once every three weeks or so she'll ask for acupuncture, and we get those points taken care of for her. I can confirm that she is a changed child. With that said, stones and oils are not the long term holistic solution. The solution is inside of you. I believe in the benefit of the bio-energies released by Mother Earth in all forms, but inside of you, you maintain the greatest ability to improve and spread love. The mental/emotional side of Chakras work as a pyramid built upon the strength of your Root Chakra, one unlocking atop the prior, but if the base is shaken, they can all experience damage or collapse, sending us back into The Dark. This is most commonly a reaction to Grief, but can happen for any host of reasons. The key is perspective and positivity as we discovered in unlocking Throat Chakra.

Love sets us free, and forgiveness liberates us from pain. As an Empath, you have the ability to connect more readily, and may have the opportunity to experience unconditional love via The Third Eye Chakra. This is a level of divinity and peace few recognize, but please turn the corner from fear and distrust in your gifts, and realize they house your ability to better the human existence for all. You have the ability to feel all people, some much more than others, but you understand best the state of human society. Your ability to affect society is profound, like a lighthouse on a rocky shore for those lost at sea to navigate by. Once you have realized your ability, you may find compassion for all life, and find cause in the peace that comes with alleviating the suffering of others. You'll feel the relief of bringing others up, and this in return will strengthen you as well. This reality is not something that most can imagine, but as an Empath you are nearly there.

I hope that you are able to see the potential behind getting stronger. Once aligned with positivity, the negative energies have little effect on you because you are counterbalancing with positivity, which is much stronger, leaving you far less susceptible, as an Empath, to the negativity of others. The answers to growth and strength are not out there for you to purchase, they are inside you to discover and grow. This growth may be painful because any weaknesses will be the point of attack, but this is a benefit because your pain lets you know where to concentrate your efforts. This will be an ever-changing challenge, but by seeing the opportunity in it you'll become ever stronger for the efforts you provide. Struggle creates strength, and weaknesses will be the target to make you stronger. The process to reach a point of enlightenment is most simply a choice based upon your awareness and intention to do so. Many people don't ever make it out of The Dark, but in gaining the courage to read this text you have already found a path. You just need to personalize this as your own.

Above, within The Third Eye profile, I mentioned that these individuals are able to communicate in the simplest of terms. As Yin and Yang would denote, there is an inherent conflict. If someone is, through enlightenment, communicating within the simplest of terms, they may state something such as "Love Thyself" (Yin). This seems so common sense that it requires no more explanation, but the path to the true meaning of this statement is far more complex when left without explanation, and the phrase does not hold the gravity necessary to inspire change. This is why story tellers of old through all cultures encapsulate messages in stories. There is a conflict within story as well, for the complexity inherent in writing or story lends itself to misinterpretation and justifications for self-fulfilling or violent action on the part of people in The Dark. Then the very explanation that was intended to explain "Love Thyself" is warped and used for ill intent (Yang). Please seek out your personal story that aligns with "Love Thyself." If it is personal, then there is no means of misinterpretation.

HEALTHY LIVING

The sad truth is, if we do not take the time to focus on wellness now, we will be forced to focus on illness later. Which would you rather do, focus on diet and exercise (mental and physical), putting those hours in at the gym and within meditative practice, or spend equal or greater hours in doctor offices' waiting rooms later, where the recovery is much harder and the costs much higher? The tradeoff is that simple and that inevitable. My general rule of thumb when considering diet: Through eating, we take in the Sun, Rain, and Earth. Ask yourself how many middlemen are between those elements and the food that you are eating. The fewer degrees of separation, most likely the healthier it is for you.

Healthy living seems to become more difficult every day, because it's less about coping and more about daily choices that reinforce our body's needs. This takes more time and effort than the quick fix coping mechanisms readily found online. Although those ideas are often valid, they are relatively impermanent in comparison to a healthy body and mind. The choice is ultimately about quantity and quality of life. For Empaths, it's specifically a choice of mental balance and wellbeing.

The trouble is, in order to truly be healthy and aware of our body's potential, we need to partially abstain from being part of the marketing and consumer culture. We are a society of addiction and habit. This starts with food and seeps into medication. Most of these centers around sugar and our society's addiction to it. Sugar is naturally occurring, but if you don't know how to get it in a healthy way, and fall victim to marketing, you'll find yourself addicted. Healthy sugars are in fiber-bound sources. These include fruits and vegetables, seeds, nuts, and whole grains. Sugars that we should try to avoid are all things that are not fiber-bound and fall under the umbrella of refined carbohydrates. This includes most cereals, breads, and chips (potatoes are a poor representative of a vegetable). If something is fiber-bound, then it takes calories to break down. Some or all of the immediate energy provided by the sugar is used in this process. A food like celery takes more energy to break down than you receive in calories, thus it is known as a negative calorie food. Fruits and vegetables also have Phyto molecules that help to balance our body. It's not as much what you eat that is important, it's what you get from the foods you take in that is important.

Chinese Medicine breaks down the effects on the body in the following way, basing illness in imbalances within Dampness, Phlegm, and Heat. Heat can be caused by consuming carcinogens or by creating an acidic, hostile environment within the body. Examples of items that cause this reaction are alcohol, smoking, and anger (adrenaline). Dampness is a retention of water or inflammation that causes puffiness. Examples of items that cause this reaction are high salt intake, stress, and sugar, which has a direct link to Diabetes. Phlegm can also be seen as retention of fluid, but is more aptly described as stuff that causes clogged tubes. Examples of these effects on the body are snot, high cholesterol, and obesity.

Histamine laden foods, such as alcohol, chocolate, red meat, matured cheese, and wine (all high in histamines due to the aging process), can overflow in the liver and create a general reaction of irritability. The liver's ability to maintain histamine levels is very important in mood and irritability. If histamine overwhelms the liver's ability to maintain healthy levels, it will keep you up at night, cause wheezing and itching, and give you heartburn. Antihistamines can help, but diet change is most effective. Furthermore, there is a significant histamine link to liver failure and seizures.

Sugar is an ineffective energy source; the effects of sugar in our diet are the opposite of grounding, as it makes us manic, then we crash, and again turn to sugar for the quick rush. The life cycle of sugar peaks at 30 to 45 minutes and then begins to fade, so we are always trying to restock. Sugar and caffeine in high amounts also cause brain fog. Studies have also found that sugar is more addictive than cocaine. As if that isn't enough, cancerous tumors feed on sugar. I believe the cancer crisis is caused by the current state of nutrition and the Standard American Diet (SAD). I find the acronym sadly ironic. The food pyramid as it exists today puts sugar, and all things that break down to glucose, at the very top.

As a society, it's easy to buy into this theory because those food items are also less expensive than fresh fruits, vegetables, and meats. These carbohydrates are complimented with a host of artificial preservatives, colors, and chemicals that can cause imbalance and sickness. There have been specific links to ADHD and food coloring. Sugar also causes inflammation in the body. All things that break down to glucose are foods that will shorten the quantity and quality of life.

The pharmaceutical industry has all kinds of solutions for people who consume a sugar rich diet. There are anti-inflammatories, pain medication, insulin for diabetics, medications to reduce blood pressure, stabilize mood, and control heart issues. I've always joked, but am surprised that pharmaceutical companies are not in the chips, cereal, and cookies business so that they could capitalize on the same target demographic twice. If looking to make an immediate change, a great way to start eating clean is to cut soda/pop out of your diet. A well-fed mind and body are a healthy mind and body.

Many Empaths can feel the energies in their foods, and this has been a factor in choosing a vegetarian or vegan lifestyle. A positive diet includes fresh vegetables; it's said that eating root vegetables and mushrooms is a form of grounding. Root vegetables, such as onion and garlic, have been shown to reduce phlegm. It has also been said that eating a diet rich in antioxidants helps to clarify your intuition. These can be found in high concentration in pomegranate and blueberries. Also worth noting, all berries, seeds, and nuts are super foods. These foods all contain a compact nutrient base.

Hydration: It's important to stay hydrated, as it promotes detoxification of the body, supports the organ systems, and helps to balance your mind.

Mind: The mind is 60% fat, and in order to have balance in the mind you must feed it. Fat feeds the mind, breaks down slowly for maintained energy, and when healthy fats such as avocados are paired with leafy greens, mushrooms, and dark berries, there is a boost to the immune system. The low-fat diet can affect your mental clarity, if taking in sugar and limiting fats. A noteworthy supplement that feeds the mind is MCT oil. It's derived from coconut oil, and feeds the mind in addition to triggering ketosis.

Qi: If you are feeling lethargic and like you are not clear, you may want to consider an increase in your Qi through diet. Recommended choices include astragalus root, ginseng root, black dates, and licorice. Hemp seed (CBD) oil also deserves mention, it's a volatile subject in Western Medicine due to hemp's recent acceptance in mainstream society. With that said, Chinese Medicine has been using hemp for thousands of years, with aged texts stating that hemp "frees the spirit and lightens the body." It works through cannabinoid receptors, assisting in the regulation of the organ systems and immune system by reducing tissue damage and inflammation. Hemp has been used in Chinese Medicine to treat pain, mental illness, seizures, and spasms. I wanted to include it in this text, as there has also been a strong correlation drawn between CBD oil and acupuncture, as they work well in tandem, promoting Qi.

Sleep: Get a full eight hours of sleep. There have been numerous studies stating that getting enough sleep assists in positive energy levels, memory, and emotional and mental clarity. Interestingly enough, Australian Aboriginal culture places great importance on dreaming. They believe that all that is created was done so within an immaterial dreamscape prior to being materialized in our world. You are conceived in this space prior to birth, and this is where you return after death. It's interesting, because if we are not able to dream, we are not able to create, because everything that is manifested in our world would first have to be conceived in a dream. Think of the self-limiting factors of not being able to dream in this cultural context. The most interesting thing about this is that there is scientific proof that thought can affect and manipulate subatomic particles, making this correct. Paired with our natural tendency to want to be correct, we do manifest our own path.

False Energy: Feeding the mind involves taking out false or ineffective energy sources. False energy is derived from stimulants such as caffeine and sugar. Caffeine has a half-life of six hours, so it's effective but addictive, and there is a significant crash.

Sobriety: Sobriety plays into this as well, for obvious reasons. If we are to purposely become imbalanced, how can we hope to be of balanced mind? Damaging effects are true of all drugs, but alcohol specifically increases the heat of a body, and can fundamentally exhaust your Qi, undermining your spirit. As is true with any drug, long term use will cause a host of further medical issues.

Collagen: Feeding our electrical system, which is made up of fascia takes collagen, is imperative. If you cannot transmit, you cannot thrive. Maintaining this system requires collagen, and due to the refined food sources that we consume, we no longer get much of it in our diet. The human body does not produce as much collagen after the early twenties, and I've seen great gains in ability once I started supplementing collagen. It's necessary in conducting and maintaining your signal, and allows you control. Taking in collagen allows us to strengthen our electrical system and gain bandwidth so that we may better disperse our energy. If we are stronger, then we are less apt to receive the energy of others. In other words, greater power and wider bandwidth of our signal can help to drown out the electrical noise of others. This also gives us greater control over our own signal and greater ability to impact others with our positivity. This goes back to Chinese Medicine, where they used the ground up hooves of donkeys to treat inflammatory disease. Since beginning to supplement collagen and healthy brain fats via MCT oil I've noticed greater clarity and ability to roll with the punches of being an Empath.

ZEN

I wanted to include this section because Zen has no terms. It's tied to no religion, stems from Sanskrit, is based in Eastern Philosophy, and derives from the Japanese word meaning meditation. Zen is, in essence, a centered concentration in the present. Simply doing anything with a focused concentration of mind leads the way to meditation as a practice of health and wellness. A simple focus in life, to live in the here and now without the anchor of the past (Bricks) or the imagination of the future (Balloons), living for the moment, the present, and all contentment therein. Zen is truth, the knowledge and acceptance of your personal oneness with all nature, living with nature harmoniously and with an inner peace.

We are all born of the same energy, and the product of our lives makes that energy our own, gives it a signature, but it does not change its source or its connection to its source...nature. Through nature, we are all connected, and any seemingly apparent or convenient separation is false or illusion. Adopting a positive attitude about the events of our life allows us great latitude to exercise choice in positivity and how we embrace the world. This personal philosophy of life has a karmic law associated with it, to put positivity into the world, positivity shall be returned.

Next time something happens to you that the old you would consider awful, flip it, and find the positive. In reality, the choice is to see it as an accident or as good fortune. Maybe it's something small, like you broke a nail. Instead of being angry that your nails no longer match, think of it as a new beginning or lesson learned, because after all, it's an opportunity to strengthen the nail again, and maybe get a new color or design. A good buddy of mine just had his sedan totaled. I've always known this guy to be in a truck. He worked through his dismay very quickly and now is back to driving a truck. He made the necessary adjustment, saw the positive in the situation, and is happier for it. It's about the perspective, attitude, and frame that we put on things. Being happy is most simply the choice to be happy. Things will be hard some days, but by focusing on the positive, we free ourselves from the unnecessary anguish that negativity holds over our mental and physical health.

The way I've put it in this book is to walk through the fire. Fire is, yes, filled with warmth and light, but takes on a thought of unpleasantness (that's for the sceptics). Once in, around, and through the fire, you'll come to find that you've not been burnt at all, but rather thawed from a frigid existence in The Dark. The Dark is a cold and unforgiving place.

Another way I look at it is that life will inevitably pass, and I've lost a lot of people close to me. Instead of seeing the negative in this, I recount all of the positive things that I had witnessed them do. I explore all of the people that they touched, the smiles they gave, the touch of their hand. I forgive myself and them for any wrongdoing, and release them. This frees them, and me, from any negativity. I find myself ever more in love with them, as I know their energy still courses through the world, resonating within me still. Once forgiven, they find me. It's simply beautiful.

You are connected to the ultimate truths of nature and wellness. You have a direct connection to the wellness of society. I'll let you know a secret: every circumstance is in balance for the wellness of you and all nature. The hardship that befalls you is to make you stronger so that you can be in your natural state, and your gift can balance out so much of the negativity of the world. This is a very big positive for you as an Empath; you are naturally capable of compassion that others perceive as unobtainable. Strong, beautiful, and bold, it takes but one small light in this world to counterbalance so much dark, because dark cannot exist in the presence of light.

Positivity brings about the means to change. What this means is that if you are going to try and make a change in your life, and you are inconsistent in your projected outcome or your ability to maintain positivity, the change will fail. If you intend to change, a steadfast positivity will provide you with all tools and resources necessary to make the change come to a point of success, because you create your whole reality.

Stress (happiness or unhappiness) is born from an internal negative attitude towards a situation, and can only be changed with a different positive and freeing viewpoint of the situation. We create our own stress. If a situation is put upon us and we react with negativity, we have in fact created the very stress that we know is bad for our mental and physical wellbeing. If we look upon the same situation and free ourselves of the unnecessary burden of stress, then we will maintain our health and wellness through positivity. This effort is not in vain, for the result is that nothing gets left out: nothing left out of your awareness, nothing left out of your practice, nothing left out of your heart, and, maybe most importantly, nothing left unsaid or unforgiven. Doing this with a centered concentration is Zen.

A LESSON FROM BUDDHA

"We are what we think"

Buddha is someone that we can all look to as an example of an enlightened Empath. In my humble opinion, the lessons provided by Buddha are the most tangible of all of the original saints of religion. Buddha's message remains the least corrupted by the mis interpretive greed of society due to its simplicity. The basic purpose of Buddhism is; it is an individual's duty to seek out people of suffering, and through compassion send them positivity.

"The stronger you become, the more gentile you must be".

-Buddha

The creed of Buddha is, the cause of pain and suffering is ignorance; it is an individual's duty to be compassionate to yourself and others, and to create positivity to light them both. The foundation of the theory is, to make any concern better, you must first understand its root cause. Without understanding the root cause, we will be subject to cravings. Cravings are described as greed, hatred, and delusion. Greed is obtaining more than needed. Hatred is an aversion to pain, both mental and physical. Delusion is an ignorance to the present and current reality. These roots are the source of addiction, and a betrayal of the virtue of our mind's truth. Without our roots, we are prone to chasing. Chasing experiences, always looking for that next rush, will inevitably end in a crash and a feeling of loss. This may leave an individual happy in a moment, but void of true sustainable happiness.

Your happiness is your responsibility. First, compassion to the self is necessary, as your life is your direct responsibility. This compassion then extends to all life you come in contact with. It's not a selfish act to self-nurture; through personal wellness, you are actually counterbalancing the

150

unwell and providing a great gift to all life, because happiness is contagious and addictive. Buddha believed the cause of all pain and suffering is a personal lack of educated awareness (ignorance). This speaks to the education process that anyone who wants to gain enlightenment must go through (walk through the fire). Internalize the positive; take a moment and savor the good in your day. Our brains are naturally wired to hang onto the negative, so it's required that we concentrate on imprinting on the positive. The good news is, you may allow yourself to begin walking your path from wherever you are.

Buddha, upon enlightenment, came upon these three pillars: Virtue, Mindfulness, and Wisdom;

Virtue (Self-regulation) – To live in an honest, humble way, without greed or want powering the mind. Monitoring actions and words to not harm yourself or others.

Mindfulness (Learning) –To make a point of understanding external experiences and how they process internally. Knowing your reactions, the why, and being able to calm the mind to respond not with impulsivity, but rather patience, compassion, and understanding. Utilizing meditation and pursuing a state of emptiness in the here and now, for this state of mind creates space for divinity where inspiration is found. This patience and calm foster the peace and joy in life.

Wisdom (Choice) – The application of Virtue and Mindfulness to ease the suffering of yourself and others through compassion and forgiveness. To realize and protect your connection to all living energy.

MEDITATION – FINDING INTUITION

Meditation defined; Reaching a state of now. Being centered, empty, and singular in the moment.

"If we could thank ourselves, the tendencies in the world would also change. As a man changes his own nature, so does the attitude of the world change toward him."

-Mahatma Gandhi

I see this quote as a beautiful representation of Karma. You attract what you radiate, so if you have fear and guilt of being an Empath, those who have fear and guilt in their lives will be drawn to you. Soon enough, you feel not only your own fear and guilt, but also the fear and guilt of those around you. Buddha segmented this under hate as an aversion to mental and physical pain, I much prefer this definition of hate, as it puts the onus on the judgmental. If you change your perception through the path of honesty and forgiveness internally, you will attract those who are honest and forgiving, relieving yourself of external hate. It is up to you to change the situation that you are 100% responsible for, and if you choose to diminish the hate in your life, the reality of your pain will also change.

Meditation has become a solution to just about everything, and for good reason, but even when you have practiced for a decade you can feel like you haven't mastered it. For the purposes of this text, I'm going to recommend a shortened version that can yield amazing results with little time disruption. We are busy, which is commonly the largest obstacle, but even if it's for a minute each day we should make the effort to meditate. Make small positive changes daily, and the mental awareness of those changes spool up over time, building great change in the mind.

I'm going to again mix cultures by recommending Ho'oponopono, the Hawaiian practice of forgiveness and healing, as a baseline for daily meditation. The primary reason being that you don't have to stop what you are doing to meditate and try to root out an issue. With Ho'oponopono you are addressing the trauma in real time as it comes up. You address each with the following phrase of compassion and kindness: I'm sorry, forgive me, thank you, I love you! Upon Ho'oponopono we can build in some basic meditation exercises and create a real time meditation around immediate feeling and response, neutralizing them past, present, and future.

When a thought comes to mind, position your spine straight. Breath in a manner where inhalation and exhalation are approximately the same duration of about five seconds, with five second holds in-between. I like to start with a breath in on "I'm sorry" (Five seconds in, like you are breathing in through a straw), (Hold for five seconds concentrating on your why message associated with the intrusion). Breath out on "forgive me" (Five seconds through a straw), (Hold five seconds, again concentrating on the why message), breath in on "thank you" (Continued progression), hold, and breath out on "I love you" (Continued progression). It also helps to imagine the sensation that you are breathing through your heart. This thought engages your heart in the exercise and increases the effects of the meditation for you and your peers, as the resonance of your heart and pericardium amplify the message internally and externally.

Although it does not fit the classical image of meditation, it truly is meditation. Moreover, it works tremendously well to address the real time stress that you are feeling within the frame of one minute. Over time and practice you'll find that your outlook begins to change. One of the most surprising things about this is that your internal communication will also start to change. I still remember the day where I complimented myself internally and I simply responded with "Thank you, I love you" as there was no reason to apologize or ask forgiveness. There is no better feeling than operating in confidence and love to the point where your internal dialogue is complimentary. I want this for you.

If you would like to take in a deeper form of meditation, try this simple meditation exercise. Sit, stand, or lay in a comfortable position with a straight spine. Touch your fingers together, focusing on the circular energy through your body between your finger points. Focus on your breath (In, hold, out, hold, in, hold, out, hold). Try to elongate these breaths to make them deeper. Do this for five minutes, focusing on finger touch points and breath. If you find your mind wandering, gently bring it back to focusing on finger points and breath. You may notice that you can feel the energy transfer between your finger points, and once ingrained into the subtle movements of your body, breath, and energies, you may feel a gentle warming and numbness.

This is living in the here and now, and you have just experienced Zen. Proficiency means peace and joy in what may be a seemingly chaotic world. What you have just felt is the oneness inside yourself: intuition. As part of the greater whole, this energy is how you fit into the larger scale of the universe: the spirit inside you, and greater connections to nature.

To take this a step further, enlightenment is a personal knowing of how one's personal energy fits into the collective energy of nature, and further knowingness of the lack of separation between the self and the collective. The suggestions provided here are simply a template; there is no wrong way to partake in meditation, so whatever way you have found that works for you is the right way.

An established story about Zen puts this in perspective. Look upon the moon within a reflective pool; when we are too busy, and the ripples of the stones cast by our lives are upon the water, we cannot see the moon clearly.

We must provide a little space and time for the ripples to dissipate, so the pool will become still and the moon will once again come into focus. This is Zen, Meditation, and Intuition. It doesn't matter how we define it, it only matters that we pause to practice.

As a personal example, I'm a swimmer, and I meditate during the endless miles that I swim. I know many athletes like me that celebrate their oneness in this way. Meditation is commonly achieved within endurance athletics, and this oneness may be explored in nature through walking, running, biking, swimming, etc... I've long said that finding your cardio of choice is a practice in meditation and longevity in wellness. Athletes strengthen the mind and body alike. It's also true that you can change your mind through compassion, kindness, and positivity, the way an athlete changes their body through interval, endurance, and weight training. They can be mutually exclusive, or combined through individual pursuit.

Concerning grounding, as defined above, it's concentration on something and it enlightens your senses. There are many well-known practices for this, but what you choose should be immediately accepted and personal to the core. A profound example of grounding is through the Tibetan culture, where Monks practice chant. They believe that tuning their vibration (Toning) through song and chant opens up meditative channels and balances their Chakra. Through this practice they are tapping into meditation, and within the practice, their intuition. Intuition is said to be the space between imagination and perception. It's the pause within the storm where we can see truth clearly. It's why there's common recommendation towards meditation, those brief moments in the day where we find calm and balance within the hustle of the day really matter. In those moments we are tapping into intuition, finding truth, and in Western terms, trusting our gut.

STEPS/DAILY PROCESS

What was good about today? I'll commonly ask my children this question to change the way that they look at the day. It's a great thing to ask when you tuck children in at night, to end their day with a positive focus.

I want you to infuse your daily life with imagery that can help you become self-loving. We all have an innate ability to care for our young. I would like for you to imagine yourself as an infant and quite helpless. Imagine yourself holding this child, eyes full of wonder and ready to experience all the beauty that the world has to offer. Feel their breath, listen for their heartbeat, enjoy their soft coo, that amazing scent coming from the top of their head, and little toothless smile.

Now imagine that you are the grown adult caretaker for this child. You are the one responsible for soothing, playing with, feeding, and, yes, changing (cleaning up the messes) in this baby's life. This baby (you) needs self-care, confidence, strength, and it is up to you to provide it as the caretaker. Feel the responsibility. It's not heavy, but only the expectation of an infant, and you have the strength to fulfill this expectation. It's the choice to sooth yourself as you would an infant. This does not mean talking down at them, but rather bringing them up. We are always encouraging our little ones to talk and walk, and the pride we feel at their accomplishments should be the same pride you feel, as if you walk out on stage and give that big speech. In daily practice, keep the imagery of a swaddled infant (yourself) in mind, and care for your heart and mind as that image expects.

Imagine if you raise this child to not react without thought, and to pause the pain caused by overreaction and impulse. It's important to realize that pain is inevitable in life, but suffering at the hand of that pain is a choice, and as such is ultimately optional. Take this forward and put a pause for thought in your physical and mental pain prior to response or reaction. This will save you from many of the self-created problems that you may face in this world. We can accomplish this through observation and listening, allowing you to understand your reactions prior to response. Others will see you as a better communicator if you take time to listen. I once heard it said, "Humans have two ears, two eyes, and one mouth, but rarely use them in proportion." Take a moment to listen, see, and then, when there is little time remaining, take the time to speak at a one to five ratio. You'll be wiser in your words, and your message will be better received for your efforts.

Below is a model progression of this change. If you choose to, you could use these as a step program. It takes twenty-one days to create a positive change or habit in your life, and only three days to break it. This means that you need to be patient with yourself, and if you choose to take these on as steps you need to give yourself the flexibility to work them over time, giving yourself adequate time to make each a habit. If you were to successfully implement one each month, then within two years you could reach a much higher state of consciousness, and escape the feelings and reactions that are real to you now. To set a realistic expectation I don't know anyone who has reached enlightenment in that short a timeframe. A near death experience is the potential exception, as these experiences have been documented to cause this type of jump in enlightenment.

In my case, I did experience a jump, but not due to a near death experience, although the difference between my prior and current existences required a death of sorts. I do feel that my ample time in The Dark was death in comparison to my time in The Light. My jump was after a seven-year depression and another eleven years of half-life (Katabasis). It then happened in a moment of realization and choice after a graced moment that I still denied and ran from for three years. I documented this story in my autobiography

(*Saved with Honu*). My story took about 20 years between the beginning of my depression to the moment where I started to dig out, and for the last nine years, with a focus on self-discovery, care, and education, I've been operating outside of The Dark. I still don't feel that I've reached true enlightenment, but it's a daily practice to be better. As I mentioned earlier, I want to shorten this for you.

Here are the steps that I've devised within my research and experience that will help us all reach The Light, if not lead us to enlightenment.

1. As an Empath, I have the will, courage and power to take charge of my life, and to stop being dependent on drugs, alcohol, and unhealthy relationships as a way to cope with my Empathic abilities.

2. I understand that my Empathic abilities are a gift provided through a spirit that is within me. My gift was given so that I may be able to help others. I must become strong enough. I will dedicate right now to helping myself, with the assistance and strength of the spirit.

3. I will become the most honest version of myself. I will be truthful with myself, and with others in a compassionate and respectful way.

4. I will see my Empathic abilities as a positive. I believe in myself, and being an Empath is a positive part of me. I know their power, and that they can be used to help other people without harming me. Furthermore, I understand that both negativity and positivity are addictive. I choose positivity.

5. I will write down and share with a trusted ally all things that make me feel shame or guilt. I understand that these feelings hold me in The Dark, and I choose, with humility and courage, to move to The Light. If you don't have anyone, shoot me an email with the

subject "Trusted confidant" (FeltItInMyHeart@gmail.com)

–All communications will remain confidential.

6. I will practice with Ho'oponopono, "I'm sorry, forgive me, thank you, I love you," when I have a memory that causes me pain. I will rejoice upon self-praise with "Thank you, I love you."

7. I am willing to try new things, as I realize my past choices do not define me, but my current choices set the foundation for my future.

8. I will enjoy my strengths, gifts, talents and creativity, and not diminish these to appease others.

9. I will let go of any negative attitudes that hold me in The Dark, such as shame or guilt.

10. I will make a list of people I harmed, and those who have harmed me. I will take the time to forgive them, myself, and (If safe to do so) have respectful, compassionate conversations to clear all negative energies. Grief will no longer hold me in The Dark, as all have been forgiven.

11. I will express love and appreciation to others and take care of the relationships that I have. Additionally, I will seek out healthy relationships with people who believe in what I seek, to support my goals and aspirations, and to make them not only possible, but probable.

12. I will make a daily effort to have compassion for, and exhibit kindness to, groups of people that I personally have not aligned with in the past.

13. I will trust my senses and take a positive viewpoint on all experiences. I will accept challenges such as Empathic moments

courageously. I will learn from each while finding the positive and my personal strength within the experience.

14. I will pause for just a moment to strategize my reaction to all things. In this moment, I will analyze the potential positive, and if a response is required, I will respond with compassion and patience.

15. I will promptly and honestly admit, seek to rectify, and apologize for my mistakes, but will not take ownership of or apologize for the mistakes of others or diminish myself.

16. I will seek out jobs, sports, and hobbies that I enjoy, confirm my ability, enforce my feelings of self-worth, and utilize my talents.

17. I will make strides to heal my body through diet, activity and exercise. I will maintain positive attitudes, organize my life, reduce stress through choice, and I will have fun.

18. Once I am fully honest and have made amends, I will cut cords with those people and behaviors that don't fully support, or that don't align with my ability or stability to always be positive.

19. I will try to find my personal calling and take steps to follow my passion. I am allowed to have a dream and to follow it.

20. I accept that there will be highs and lows in my life, but I will approach both with a positive attitude, realizing the opportunity to learn and grow stronger in each. I will smile each time upon this realization, and internally acknowledge my positivity towards the challenge. "Thank you, I love you."

21. My awareness and Empathic abilities will grow into an innate strength where I realize my positive connection to all living things. I will take steps to provide balance, joy, love, and peace to the world through my gifts and actions.

DEVELOP A PERSONAL CODE OF CONDUCT

It's important to develop a general set of rules to help you navigate through sticky situations, because as we stray away from absolute statements based in emotion, things can become a bit more grey, and decisions that used to be automatic slow in process. It's nice to have a code of conduct in these situations so that we can quickly remind ourselves what we stand for. This is a creed or set of rules that you make with yourself as to how you will continue from this day forward. I'll share mine with you as an example, because it helped me to become who I am today. I encourage you to write your own, because everyone's past is different, and how we move past the things anchoring us in our past is personal and unique.

My first ten rules I've had for some time, and they were published previously in my autobiography. I'm happy to say that they have stood the test of time, and I honor them daily. The last two are more recent, and have come from realizations due to moving through the steps above, my writings, conversations, and continued efforts to be better. It just goes to show that these things should be expected to change through life as you grow and develop.

My rules;

1. "Don't be that guy" - I spent a lot of time as "that guy," and we all know that guy. He/She is the one that is over-compensating in some way, attempting to run from the hurt that they are feeling. Please be patient with these people and take some time to listen, they will surprise you. They need something to believe in, and often it's just out of reach. Remind them to believe in themselves, or just give them a compliment. If you find yourself here please

remember, you don't have to be everything to everyone; start by being enough to support yourself.

2. "Control your controllables" - The things that are within your control, take care of them. If it falls outside of your realm, for the love of yourself let it go. You will be better for it. Worrying about things that you can't control is a sure-fire way to lose health and gain stress. A great way to start this is by giving five compliments a day; it's within your control, and will help both yourself and others.

3. "Enjoy the things that you can do" - I was in a body cast and still found a way to use a swing set. Life is not all bad; find something that you enjoy.

4. "Finish your thoughts with a positive" - The root of it is, if you are complaining to yourself, you will create outward negativity. Finish your thoughts with a positive; you may change your perspective, and consequently your world.

5. "Do the work/follow through/be reliable" - No one else is going to do it for you. Your reward is the one you make. The reliability is your work ethic, and remember that relationships take work, too. Be reliable to those who love you, and who you love in return. Here is where your decisions, honesty, and actions define you.

6. "Eat with a purpose" - Out of all of them this is probably the most difficult. Eating for taste is often the wrong reason. Try nutrition instead, as you will live longer and happier.

7. "Find something cardio that you can love" - Stay active in one way or another. Do something that ignites calorie burn within your body, and your mind will be happier and more productive.

8. "Don't get stuck" - This is about finding happiness in what you do. If you feel stuck, then find something that makes you happy. Caveat: children will slow you down, but they will not make you stuck; you are forced to progress alongside them, so it's continuous motion in a forward direction. It's magical to be a part of. Another form of getting stuck is being in a continual cycle of admiration of the things you have accomplished. If you get stuck here, you'll fail to do great things in the future.

9. "Don't take yourself, or your environment, too seriously" - If you take the world that you live in too seriously, then you may just lose the ability to enjoy the little things. If you are a stick in the mud, you will get stuck. Be light hearted, and others will be attracted to your sense of wellbeing. Make fun of yourself, and let your flaws be known. You'll be stronger for it.

10. "Never stop learning" - Especially from your children. Let's not kid ourselves. Time does not stand still, and we are getting older. As we get older, we fall further out of touch with what is fueling the world, and will become more complacent in our ways. If you truly want to stay young at heart, always learn the lessons that your children are experiencing. You may have had the answer to the challenge twenty years ago, but the societal context around the challenge has evolved. Working through the challenge as it pertains to today's challenges will make you a generation younger, in thought and by association.

11. My Aunt Jodee once said, "Always side with the one that does not get a vote." - I've found such profound wisdom in this statement. Firstly, it's Empathic in its core, beautiful in its practice, and compassionately loving. Imagine a world where everyone

practiced this as a rule. There would be no hate, no famine, no pain without compassion.

"Don't let your reason become your excuse" – Reasons vs Excuses can be likened to a cycle of Yin/Yang, with Reason being related to Yang resulting in action and a positive fruitful direction, and an Excuse being related to Yin and inaction. The greatest and worst parts of the of the human existence relate to our ability to imagine. Creativity is the word that we use to describe the positives (Reason driven). Anxiety is the word that we use to describe the worst parts of our imagination, as anxiety is the fear of the worst-case imagined outcome (Excuse driven). If we are always imagining the worst, then we may rob ourselves the opportunity to respond with courage, allowing those fears to stop us (Excuse). If we look at the problem as a challenge or creative opportunity, then we shall find courage and step into it (walk through the fire), taking up the opportunity (Reason). We all have reasons (electric fences) in our past. Find a pair of insulated wire cutters and break through, take action so that your reason cannot become your excuse.

IT'S UP TO YOU TO BE STRONGER

Empathy is meant to reach out, to heal, and to share in one's pain or happiness. Having a gift that allows you to do this naturally is a blessing. Prior to this all taking hold, you will need to practice a willingness to stop blaming yourself and others, and to accept responsibility for your thoughts, actions, feelings, beliefs, truths, and lies. This is a form of forgiveness, and is necessary to move forward. You want to leave behind those things in your former lifestyle that will pull you down. This can be a person, item, drug, promiscuity, music, really anything that associates itself as a negative in your former life. You must realize that only you can control you. Your outcome is not imposed upon you, but left to the choices that you make. There may be instigators in your life, but they may be removed through choosing your friends wisely. It may take a while to weed out the positive from the negative, but through listening to your body and practicing with the tools provided as needed, you will know these thought patterns, excuses, lies, and individuals. You simply need to rediscover what you already know to be true. This ability alone will lead you to a path of knowing and wisdom, and will add to an ever-compounding vision of self-love.

Compassion is necessary to achieve joy. Joy is necessary to lead. Leadership is necessary to become a healer. The great news is that, once a healer through your Empathic gift, you alone have the ability to counterbalance one million people or more who reside in The Dark. This makes you that leader, and through your progress of getting stronger, you counterbalance more and more of the evils of this world. Your strength as one who feels, knows, and who has most likely experienced the pains in this world, allows you to provide the most precious gift back to the world. This gift starts with self-love. That alone provides an uplifting ripple effect through all time and space that lifts the human experience higher. In addition, practicing self-love is important because we cannot give away what we don't have for ourselves. As an Empath, you then broadcast this as if a lighthouse on the rocky shore to all of those lost at sea. You are the Yin to all the world's Yang, and all you need to find is compassion towards yourself. This can be your purpose; this alone is enough. You are enough, and love will find you. When you love you, you'll find that love is the easiest part of being an Empath.

SELF-PROTECTION, QUICK WINS

The internet is drowning in quick-win solutions for being an Empath. The trouble is, they don't always work, and most of those that do work lose efficacy over time. With that said, they do hold value, because sometimes, even when you are strong and capable of helping others on a regular basis, that energy sticks with you, and it's nice to have quick wins to shed what is not yours.

Smudging - Smudging is very common, and most commonly consists of burning sage to clear the air of negative energy. I love that it began as a Native American practice. It's commonly used to purify a space or dispel negative energy. It's also used to create a healing state, assisting in spiritual conflict. Benefits can include better energy and improved cognition. These are important as an Empath, because sometimes smudging can clear the proverbial air (both space and state of mind).

Grounding - Grounding is, in short, doing something that you love, and/or getting back to nature or your personal home. Meditation is a means of grounding. Grounding is the practice of reminding yourself who you are and where you feel comfortable. My favorite way is to walk outside with my shoes off. Getting back to nature is a widely accepted grounding practice. Everything is rooted in the earth, and gaining that foundation in my life puts me at ease. Grounding doesn't have to be this for you; it's going to be different for everyone, because we all produce and respond to different energies. Play around with it, and gravitate to things that you love.

A permanent form of grounding is to surround yourself with good people and to provide love and assistance to those people. Getting good people to provide a permanent level of love on a physical, mental, emotional, and spiritual level is the most effective and permanent source of grounding.

Candles - Candles are used for many reasons, and the colors have specific meaning:

1. Rose/Pink - during meditation, love/romance/light

2. Turquoise – consciousness

3. White – balance, all uses

4. Blue – relieves fear and anxiety/wisdom

5. Light Blue – devotion

6. Purple – strength/ambition/psychic

7. Red – health/passion/fertility

8. Yellow – activity/imagination

9. Green – success/ambition

10. Orange – zest/change

11. Black – fights evil

Totems – Totems are a physical item that you carry with you as a reminder or focus point. Many people keep a small item to grasp or keep in their pocket. Good options are a Chakra stone of your choosing or a Chinese Hishru (Healthy Ball). The Healthy Ball was originally two simple solid metal balls and were heavy; they were later made lighter and musical by making them hollow and filling that space with sound plates incorporating high and low tones. Moving them in your hand clockwise (Moving forward – right hand) or counterclockwise (Slowing down – left hand) may provide relaxing focus and ease the mind, giving music and direction to your moment.

Another form of a totem is a tattoo. Tattoos can be grounding in the moment, but can also serve as a permanent symbolic reminder of strength and ability, allowing them to be used for grounding in the future as well. Be careful to make your tattoos personally positive. Due to their permanence, they must stand the test of time. If done with patience and love, they can be a powerful grounding block.

Heirlooms - Those things/moments that we derive meaning from don't originate as material possessions, but rather they carry an energy that is derived from the spiritual world. Think of the heirloom that has been passed down over generations in your family. Yes, this may be a material possession, but the energies of those who loved this item prior to yourself still reside in them. As love is necessary to obtain a strong and everlasting energy source, this then can bind to the items passed down. You may be attracted to it, even though you find it ugly, odd, and old, simply due to this unseen energy that relaxes and calms you, just as if the original owner were rocking you to sleep as a child. This, specifically, becomes stronger if the item was given to you in an act of love by the person with whom you feel an attachment. Love conquers all; these energies and items of love are a surviving testament. The opposite can be true as well; energy bindings can be negative, so take stock of these things as you go, and keep those that are most precious.

Living Spaces – Living Spaces are incredibly important, because we have a tendency to pick up everything in a set radius, and then with distance our sensitivity fades. This does not count for the loves of our lives, but strangers or acquaintances can be tuned out with distance. If you are living in a college dorm with 1,000 imbalanced teenagers, well, let's say that this environment is not ideal for an Empath trying to study or sleep. Then you have the spiritual aspect. I think most of us have lived in a space that retains the energies of its prior inhabitants, and, at times, the memories of those inhabitants if something shocking took place. In the case that you can own a home, I've found that picking a relatively new, or new construction home outside the city has helped me to balance.

Cardio – Many endurance athletes have reported high states of consciousness resulting in peace and joy. Medically speaking, this relates to the body's natural dopamine release system, which also reduces stress and pain. In these states, the body also releases endorphins and serotonin that have a calming effect on the organ systems, strengthening the body.

Charity – Helping others helps you. It all works equally through karma; find some way to give your time and energy; karma and dopamine will take care of the rest.

Addiction – This is a temporary fix to our Empathic nature. We are tricking the mind to shut out the torment. This is using a substance or a risky act as a form of grounding. It's no surprise that we are attracted to things that allow us secondary focus to forget it all for a while. But the addictive and destructive nature of drugs and alcohol chips away, wounding the real you, and in the process your potential and current real life.

Stop the Feed – We are finding that more and more of our lives are lived online. This is particularly damaging in times of trauma. On the flip side, sometimes we are able to find like-minded people who provide support in times of strife. In either situation, keep a personal tally. At times, it may be necessary to stop the feed. This can be as permanent or temporary as you need, but throughout this book the topic of self-care is continuous. Stopping the feed may just be the best version of self-care in the moment.

Cord Cutting (Step 18) – Cord Cutting, in my opinion, is the most painful and cathartic piece of being an Empath. There a times where we just need to separate ourselves from people in our lives, as they bring us instability and do little to provide solace. Cord cutting is a personal ceremony, conducted to separate the other party from our aura and psyche. So why is it called cord cutting? I suppose it's a euphemism for the umbilical cord and a physical separation from another being, but in the case of being Empathic, it's a mental connection, an ability to feel angst, anger, fear, uncertainty and confusion that needs to be left behind in our lives in order to truly move forward.

A guest editor of this book described them: "The cords are tendrils that go between us and anyone we have an energetic connection with. Visualize them coming from you, and then just bring them back in until they are gone. I feel an immediate difference when I do this." Larri Cook

This cord may run through your mind daily, because of a task that you need to complete, prior dialogue, a recent encounter, or a tragedy for the counterparty, or perhaps your aura may be drawing upon the connection. Cutting the cord is a personal act; it cannot be done in defiance or spite. You must personally turn the corner, and in a way of forgiveness, to cut the cord in a peaceful and healing manner. This means letting go of any score that you may have been keeping, and wiping the slate clean concerning a personal grudge that you've been holding onto. In order to free yourself of this connection, you must not live in remembrance of this; forgiveness is necessary to move forward.

A sample process:

1. Cut communicative ties with the other party.

2. You must be sober, and allow yourself to open up in a safe place. A clean and acute mind is necessary.

3. Light a candle. Any candle will do, but if you are the symbolic type light a white candle, as it represents all colors. This will cover all aspects of the connection and its Chakra.

4. Clear your mind, take away all of the hardship felt by this person, the score counting, the grudge. Mentally picture all of this inside of the flame, and take revelry as you watch it burn.

   • If you would like a literal symbol, have everything written out ahead of time. Burn the paper within the flame during the ceremony. Do this safely, having a bucket of water available to extinguish any unwanted fire.

5. In your own way, in your own words, forgive this person. Keep the imagery of your forgiveness outside of the flame. Do not write this down, as your forgiveness is meant to move with you. Forgiveness is for you, not them.

6. Mentally wrap yourself in the warmth of your forgiveness flame as the anguish and sorrow burn away. If tears come, let them flow, this is part of the forgiveness process and should not be fought.

7. When you are clear and feel the process is completed, blow out the candle. This is symbolic of your choice to cut the connection and move on. The process may take as long as you need; once the flame of the candle goes out, you are free of the conflict. If the flame of the candle goes out on its own, consider the conflict resolved.

8. At this point you are clear. The conflict has passed in the fire.

9. Hold your forgiveness tight and wrap yourself in it as needed, as this is now your light in place of the flame.

10. Grounding, grounding, grounding.

I've found through my experience with family or personal relationships that the above methods don't always stick or yield permanent results. I believe that this is due to hardline: blood is sticky, and holds connection. If this is the case, there are methods that rely on a bit more offense. If you require this type of cord cutting, I recommend you slow down the process and write a letter. Take time to write by hand, and use the postal service for delivery. We have become too quick with email, text, and digital messenger platforms. In order for this to work, you and the recipient need to be forced to read, re-read, and take in the gravity of the information prior to response. This is also a good way to separate from passed spirits.

11. Sit down and write your letter. If you want the first draft to be digital that's fine, but the sent letter should be hand-written.

12. Wait, and edit over a bit of time. This can be a week or more. It's good to be diligent. This will allow you to really sort your thoughts, and get all the pieces and parts included and in their right place.

13. Add a line or PS that summarizes that you forgive them, and release them of any responsibility towards you, and if other parties are involved who cannot represent themselves (children or the deceased), you may consider including them in that release as well.

14. Draw attention to additional details that come up prior to you sending the letter but that you feel need to be included with sticky notes, highlighting, and arrows. As a recipient, these will have a specific gravity, and will draw the eye. Sticky notes can also be removed and kept as reminders. These can be well wishing, a reminder to smile, or may draw out a painful moment in a different way of writing.

15. Request no response. Block phone number, email address, and social media as necessary.

16. Put the letter in an envelope, lick, seal, return address, stamp, and mail it. You putting in this effort, and getting it to a slow delivery system, allows you the time to close the box and begin your healing process, even before your recipient gets the mail.

17. You need not worry about some sarcastic response thirty seconds later. Most likely, the paper form and hand-writing will draw the recipient in, have a sense of permanence and gravity, and you'll finally get the closure you deserve.

If you have prior letters from your recipient, send them back. Remain courteous and professional, but this releases you from the energy associated with the prior correspondence, and reinforces the permanence of the action.

After cord cutting, it's natural to feel that there is a piece of you missing. Sometimes it's a really large piece and its loss is very unexpected. You don't have to fill this hole with other things; give it some time to mend on its own. If I'm completely honest, I have a hole so large in my heart that it feels like an unfillable void. I'm simply relieved that I know the why, how, and when, and I can reason with that most days. Remember that you chose to cut that out for a reason: your overall health and ability to move forward. One day, circumstances may align where that hole fills. Time heals, and time passed changes everything. I've found that sometimes when souls that we hold connection to pass over, the Empathic bonds release. This is because they do not operate at a level and strength to remain strong enough, and are drowned out. This can be damaging, but this can also be graceful and freeing. In my opinion, the fact that these connections can be reinforced or fickle is a good thing, and our graduation and learning from the process is the goal.

Through this book, I've shared with you some of my personal struggles and my efforts to become a healthy and balanced Empath. I want to provide the following journal entry to provide a bit more context concerning the challenge that cord cutting can be.

01/16/2018 Journal entry

"Grandpa came to sit with me today; I know it was him. In popped, 'Five foot two, eyes of blue,' the old Dean Martin song. Prior to the internet, I thought only Grandpa knew the song and all the words. He sang this sweet tune day and night, on horseback, in the old blue truck, and being that I was never more than two feet away from him I heard it all the time. Grandpa's been gone for some time. I was working under the assumption that he was reincarnated, because I'd not heard from him for years. I think this is fair, because I carried him with me through a massive depression. So why today? I actually know the answer: this last weekend I cut the Empathic cord between myself and biological father. I had to; he's built walls I cannot surmount, he's not been responsive since publish although I tried to maintain our established communication, he has missed holidays, and now has missed my eldest daughter's birthday. My daughters are old enough to ask real time questions about their emotions, and I've not received answers to like questions, so I have no way of answering them. His empathetic cry has been deafening, and I've grown weary of sheltering against it. In faithful effort to protect my daughters from the thoughts and feelings I've experienced, I severed the bond through cord cutting to the best of my ability, but have felt empty in the last couple of days."

"Then, 'Five foot two, eyes of blue,' and I smile. My world shifts to light, wonder, and I'm a kid again, leaning against grandpa, the smell of his aftershave thick in the air, snuggled between him and a saddle horn atop a horse, riding through a pasture to a slow horseback sander, with grandpa using the clip pity clop of horse hooves as a makeshift drum beat, gazing at an orange, pink and purple Nebraska sunset. All of my worries dissolving into tune, 'five foot two, eyes of blue, but oh what those five feet could do, has anybody seen my gal?' Grandpa reminds me he was Dad, he was always there, and I didn't ever want to be anywhere else, unless he was giving me a whisker burn, but even then I loved it for the long term. He did everything that I and he could imagine to make my childhood complete, along with Mom, My aunt Ann, and Grandma. I had it all, enough love to stack it to Jupiter and back. The best thing about Grandpa, he was a true believer in the old Western happy ending. I literally get to ride off into the sunset with him. I think he was just waiting for me to come home. Thank you, Grandpa, for the extremely timely reminder, and being my childhood Dad. Five foot two, eyes of blue, I love you."

I wanted to share some of my real process. You are not alone; you are not crazy; Step 18 is really tough; and you simply choose to protect this beautiful communication method that is so core to us all. I'm one of many. I struggle too, but the trying times elevate us, and it's so worth it on the other side.

ELECTRO MAGNETIC FIELD PROTECTION

EMF (Electro Magnetic Field) protection is probably the most beneficial, but least understood, subject that I'll write about in this book. The reason is the science of it all. With that said, the science is based in the balance of the human body, and therefore is helpful to an Empath. The other piece of this is that so much of the subject matter about being an Empath is written in a defensive light. This is one place where we can easily go on offense without all of the self-reflection and control. I often think that the best defense is a good offense, and that's how EMF protection works.

As established, we all produce and store energies; your bio-energy can be influenced, and these devices help to break through those barriers. EMF waves are all those electronically-created waves that have been shown to damage cells. There are natural defenses against this damage, such as tourmaline and amethyst, as they are excellent in boosting the strength of the human aura. In addition, copper is a great amplifier. This is a portion of the science that goes into EMF protection. Today, we have jewelry items available that amplify the human aura. It was found that this also protects against EMF. If we, as Empaths, are taking the time to boost and protect our own signal, this can assist in protecting us from the signals of others. This has been scientifically proven, although we've intuitively known this all along.

There are many options. I first came upon this through exposure by a great teacher of mine to a device called Qlink. The white papers on these devices are available, but the short of it is, they capture your bio-energy, store it, and amplify it. They work! I wear one over my heart/pericardium all of the time. My rule of thumb is, if I can sleep with it on, it's good. Sleeping with them on can clear your energy and reinforce your signal, somewhat like a personal dreamcatcher. You may notice an increase in your energy levels; this is well documented by Qlink. It makes perfect sense. Boost yourself, your signal, and your energy and your abilities will follow. In my experience and in wearing one every day and night for the last eight years, I've become stronger mentally and physically, and I sleep better.

There are also a host of pendants and beads available on the open market that utilize lava rock, quartz, and tourmaline, as well as other elements in an effort to provide a positive body response. They are generally marketed for EMF protection, Healing jewelry, or as Scalar energy devices. These devices most commonly operate on the theory that negative ions boost the bio-energy of the individual and protect against negative energy of EMF. My favorite items usually have a mix of hematite, which is magnetic and good for energy, mixed with Chakra stones for energy protection. I find that the protection and accumulation of energy yields a nice mix in the middle of a tough workday in the office.

Himalayan Salt Lamps work in this way as well, due to their production of negative ions. I've also found Scalar energy pendants that I use in my fitness training and sport due to the positive energy gain. I found a rather expensive bead that, in conjunction to my Qlink, provides great results for me. The energy of the additional positive energy source, combined with the Qlink storing and boosting my energy, is very powerful. Since the day that I combined the two I've been able to perform cord cutting with a level of success that was not possible prior. The great news is all of these solutions are relatively inexpensive. The Qlink is a little spendy, but worth it. If you try something used, let it cool off for a week once you receive it. Qlinks are waterproof, so submerging them in water will change the base energy as well. This will give it time to wash away the previous owner's energy.

If you are a do-it-yourself type, create your own jewelry. Great base items include copper to conduct and store, magnets (hematite) to draw in your body, crystals such as rose quartz, amethyst, and tourmaline. I've seen beautiful self-creations, and what's better than serving your own recovery and being proud of something self-created.

I debated for a long time about the inclusion of a Qlink affiliate link. For me, it's not about money. I want to use my energy in a way where I bring others up. With that in mind, I found a way to include the affiliate link and feel good about it. FeltIt InMyHeart Press also publishes children's books on a 'buy one give one' basis. I give a lot of books away with the goal of defeating illiteracy. Those books share the same fundamental messages that you've found in this book, just written for our children. Here's the deal; if you purchase a Qlink using my affiliate link, all proceeds will be treated as donation funds, and will be used to give books. These books will be purchased at cost, and given to at risk youth, with the goal of defeating illiteracy.

Thank you in advance.

https://share.shopqlink.com/730.html

HEART RATE

This is purely theory based on my own experience. I've found through wearing a heart rate monitor that I'm more empathically susceptible at heart rates between 60 Beats Per Minute (BPM) to 120 BPM. This is where the bulk of the human population operates. This leads me to think that there's secondary communication through hearts that commonly match our rate and syncopation. It's well documented that people who are deeply in love will synchronize their heart rates, and this, logically, is due to and leads to a deeper level of communication.

This leads to the theory that I don't seem as susceptible when I'm holding my heart rate under 60 BPM, as this is where I slip into a base meditative state. I think there are fewer people who can operate at this level, and thus I don't pick them up. The opposite is also true. If I'm working out, and operating within my chosen cardio sport with a heart rate above 120 BPM, my Empathic tendencies simply fade away. I think this is due to the serotonin and dopamine release that calm my organ network. In addition to this, the effects of those chemicals calm my response when I am sensitive.

Given the need for both Yin (Meditation), and Yang (Cardio), the better balanced I am with these two odds, the less time I spend in-between, and the less empathically affected I am with my time in-between. As a disclaimer, it's impossible to maintain a heart rate that does not operate between 60-120 BPM most of the time, but I've found that my time outside of the "Normal" range soothes my soul and refreshes my ability to be balanced rather than reactive.

It's also important to state that this does not work when manic. It's very possible to keep a heart rate above 120 BMP in a manic state fueled by adrenaline (Acidic). This is generally stress induced, focused on anxiety, and in place of the calming effects of dopamine and serotonin (Calming), we just get bombarded with more Empathic signals due to the chemical makeup feeding our bodies. We want to become stable in mind and body in comparison to the bulk of society so that we may better control our impulses and feelings, internal and external.

The common factor between the two of these (60/120 BPM) is breathing. Breath control is a factor in both relaxation and cardio. My cardio is swimming, so I'm generally operating in an oxygen deprivation zone during aerobic activity. Similarly, I've found that it's easiest to slip under 60 BPM when I'm controlling my breathing. I've devised a theory; I call it finding the bottom of my lungs. It's a breath control exercise where I breathe out slowly through a (virtual) straw for five seconds. This is paired with shallow breaths in for five seconds, and five second holds in between. It seems to expel the negative.

The theory is based on a swimming oxygen utilization fact that I tripped across years ago. At any given point in time we only utilize 17% of the oxygen in our lungs. This means that we can cycle off 83% of our breathing. I utilize this in swimming to maintain buoyancy, cycling off about 20% of my lung capacity and maintaining the other 80% to stay more buoyant. In meditation it's the opposite, I maintain the bottom 20%, and stay empty over the top. This is the theory of finding the bottom of your lungs. If you can do this and maintain it, then you should be more focused and less susceptible to Empathic intrusion under 60 BPM. By no means is any of this easy, and years of work may be necessary. Walking through the fire gets you to the other side where all of the rewards are.

FIND YOUR TRIBE

Animals (yes, humans are animals too; you can dress it up all you want, but we still fit this distinction) have evolved to create separation from those things that pain them. This can be in the form of physical and mental separation, but mental separation causes imbalance. It's understandable that, if you run into an electric fence once, then you'd avoid that same fence in the future. It's also understandable that, if you experience a mental trauma, then you'd avoid that circumstance in the future. The trouble with this is that humans have unbounded imagination for the "what if." The "what if" is an extrapolation of the past and imagination of a future, even if it's not based in reality. The mind can't tell the difference, so even without reality, if you convince the mind it's real, it's real. Eventually we get ourselves so wrapped up in mental electric fences that we've caged ourselves and are unable to feel, think, or move. We then describe this as anxiety, which I define as a fear of the worst case imagined outcome. This means that, as an Empath, if you have one bad experience that you naturally begin to wall those pieces of you off. Each time that you do this you are sacrificing an essential piece of who you are, and you begin to shelter yourself from the world and from your true nature.

The mind is the opportunity. Our minds are naturally wired to hold onto the bad and dispose of the good. This has been hard-wired into our DNA as a strategy for survival. Do you ever get stuck for hours reliving a moment that just passed, thinking about it? For example, we all have those "I should have said that" moments. That's great, especially if you allow it to yield a positive learning situation and courage to change moving forward. If we get stuck there, we are in single focus mode and the world is just passing us by as we lose current opportunities.

182

Stability is also an imagined state, because the world and life are always in a state of flux. We naturally see this lack of stability as a threat and are always struggling against it, even to the point of personal loss and imbalance. Stability can be found in a way through the value of social well-being and maintaining positive relationships. With that said, this very yearning is generally why we get pulled into unhealthy relationships. As Empaths, we often find ourselves putting others first and hiding ourselves away. We can also have an unhealthy fear of true relationships, because with another person in your life you may have more to feel. You may have a whole new problem set that you know you'll have a tendency to take on as your own. It's important to understand that this fear and hesitation is a natural state of mind. It's less about you and your choices than it is a hard-wired piece of you. It's been there since the days when being eaten by a saber-toothed tiger was a daily threat, so you can't get rid of it. Rather, you need to face it.

So, when you put these together, you are hard-wired to focus on the negative, avoid physical and mental electric fences, and you are yearning for stability. All of a sudden, you find yourself ordering groceries online, working from home, all your friends are online, and you would never see them in person (because then you may gain an Empathic connection, and can you really trust anyone?), your nights have no social contact outside of your favorite shows, and you never leave the house. There are days when this sounds great, but an Empath alone and without a tribe is a travesty, because we are those who are the wise healers as described in Chinese Medicine. We are the foundation of a healthy, loving society. We are the compassion that our world desperately needs.

Going back to the concept of tribe and the way we are hardwired to belong to a tribe, choice and relationships are the beauty in the situation, and relationships are both key and the source of well-being. They allow us to feel safer, as our brains are wired to live in social groups. We find safety in numbers. When we can pursue relationships without the need for Us vs Them, becoming accepting of all individuals, species, and environments, then we are able to transcend. To start, we need to understand that every fence is not an electric fence, and with a good pair of wire cutters or a big chainsaw, not every fence can hurt or contain us. The wire cutters or chain saw are self-love and compassion. Love and compassion in tandem allow us the strength to survive, find love in ourselves and others, and maintain a sense of stability through our relationships. To accomplish this, we must break down the walls. We can then look back on our past with the understanding that past pains are not truly tied to the present or future by anything other than our own minds.

The cost of our overactive imagination for everything that can go wrong is that we stop living, are plagued by anxiety, and we miss out on all of the wonderful opportunities that are in the present. We miss these opportunities because we are not taking the time to consider the positive of the original electric fence. These original fences are usually based in memories from our childhood. Yes, we got shocked, and yes it hurt, but we learned from that experience and found another way. That electric fence may have been the best thing for us, because without it we may never have earned the pair of insulated wire clippers. That tool expanded the scope of our world to get to the next fence that required the big chain saw. Now we can break through almost anything. One day you find yourself driving a bulldozer, armed with wire cutters, chainsaws, and a thermal lance, and find there are no mental barriers that you can't overcome. This toolset is a mix of compassion and courage, and with it comes true living, true freedom, because you are finding the positive in each obstacle, and simply know that you can overcome.

THE BIG PICTURE

We started this book looking to gain self-love. The word "self" was an afterthought in the title, but it's so important. The reason for this is it's impossible to give something away that you don't have for yourself. If you don't have self-love, how can you be expected to truly love others? This thought left the prior title, *Empath to Love,* incomplete. We commonly say we love others, and in small circles this is true, but enlightenment is unlimited and unconditional love of everyone. In this thought, we circle back to Us vs Them, and again begin to protect ourselves out of fear. Fear and love don't mix, so this is not enlightened love, this is The Dark tricking our minds, playing on our imagination and insecurity within ourselves.

This is why self-love is so important, because it's the key to enlightenment and your ability to live as an Empath. Is it easy? Not even a little bit. Does it get easier? Yes, in The Light and through the seeking of enlightenment. In this way, self-improvement becomes a way of existence, and teaching is a form of giving love. This is a self-fulfilling karmic wheel, as those who receive then provide. The hope of the teacher is that their message brings up the whole of the human existence, and brings balance to all living things.

I have a super short version of this that I tell my children all the time: "You create 90% of your own problems in this world." I'm sure they have an impersonation of me saying this that will survive long after I'm gone. In truth, we create 100% of our own problems, and they have even begun to look at it this way, for simply labeling something as a problem is the creation of the problem. Labeling the same situation as a challenge or opportunity then makes it a positive and takes the negative connotation away.

The greater message is this: What most people think about the causes for their reaction is actually an effect of past decisions compounded into that moment - self-punishment for past action taken or not taken. The secret is not the consequence, but the attitude towards it that makes the true impact on the happiness and fulfillment of a life. If one is to take on the challenge of a consequence with a positive attitude of change, potential, and learning, then they will inevitably walk through the fire, make amends as needed, see that it wasn't so bad, and learn from the experience in a positive way. If you believe that any event will turn out to benefit to you, it will. Perspective is truly your best ally in life, as in remaining positive you can overcome all.

I say this to my children as they are still young. I try to also instill within the message that this is not a saying meant for them/you to lead to a cautious life, but rather a saying to lead to a conscious life. Living consciously in love and forgiveness allows you true balance. Having compassion for yourself is required for healing. Having compassion for others is paying the healing you've done forward into the world. Teaching that love through thought and simplicity raises all who you touch. Teaching others to have compassion for themselves is healing the world. Teaching others to have compassion for others changes the world.

"If you have come to help me, you are wasting your time. If you have come because your liberation is bound up with mine, then let us work together."

-Lilla Watson – Aboriginal Elder – Australia

I hope you now understand why this book was written with this quote in mind. Empaths, let's go change the world, I'm here with you.

Much Love,

Arlo

www.ingramcontent.com/pod-product-compliance
Lightning Source LLC
Chambersburg PA
CBHW031547040426
42452CB00006B/225